ZEPPO'S FIRST WIFE

ZEPPO'S FIRST WIFE

NEW AND SELECTED POEMS

GAIL MAZUR

THE UNIVERSITY OF CHICAGO PRESS
Chicago and London

GAIL MAZUR is the author of four earlier books of poems, the most recent of which, *They Can't Take That Away from Me,* was a 2001 finalist for the National Book Award. She has been awarded fellowships from the National Endowment for the Arts and the Bunting Institute (now the Radcliffe Institute). Distinguished Writer in Residence in Emerson College's Graduate Program in Writing, Literature and Publishing, she is the founding director of the Blacksmith House Poetry Series in Cambridge, Massachusetts.

The University of Chicago Press, Chicago 60637
The University of Chicago Press, Ltd., London
© 2005 by The University of Chicago
All rights reserved. Published 2005
Printed in the United States of America

14 13 12 11 10 09 08 07 06 05   1 2 3 4 5

ISBN: 0-226-51447-1 (cloth)

Library of Congress Cataloging-in-Publication Data

Mazur, Gail.
     Zeppo's first wife : new and selected poems / Gail Mazur.
        p.   cm. — (Phoenix poets)
     ISBN 0-226-51447-1 (cloth : alk. paper)
     I. Title. II. Series.

PS3563 .A987Z34 2005
811'.54—dc22

                                          2005043095

⊚The paper used in this publication meets the minimum requirements of the American National Standard for Information Sciences—Permanence of Paper for Printed Library Materials, ANSI Z39.48-1992.

Contents

THEY CAN'T TAKE THAT AWAY FROM ME (2001)

THE COMMON (1995)

From THE POSE OF HAPPINESS (1986)

***From* NIGHTFIRE (1978)**

Acknowledgments

Grateful acknowledgment is made to the periodicals in which these poems, some in slightly different versions, first appeared:

AGNI: "At First, They"
AGNI Online: "The Swamp Trail"
Granary Books/Pressed Wafer: "Rudy's Tree"
Ploughshares: "Blue Umbrella"
Provincetown Arts: "Cape Air"
Salamander: "Black Ducks (Poem Ending with a Line of Su Tung-P'o),"
        "Night Visitation," "Queenie"
Salmagundi: "Acadia," "Cemetery Road," "Dana Street, December,"
        "September," "To X"
Slate: "American Ghazal," "Enormously Sad" (© 2004 Microsoft Corporation)
TriQuarterly: "A Small Door" (as "Door"), "To Whoever May Be Concerned:"
        "Waterlilies," "Zeppo's First Wife"
Women's Review of Books: "Now:"

*

Special thanks to LS and RP for their exhilarating support and advice, and, always, to MM for his love and his art.

New Poems

Enormously Sad

What a small feeling the phrase *enormously sad*
alludes to this morning—a child has turned
away, or, you sense defeat, the grief and defeat
of disappointed love, failed friendships, defeat
of work come to nothing. Grief and defeat
pervade the kitchen, the bedroom, the walk
downstairs to the laundry, pervade the basket
of unloved socks and charmless underwear,
and the arms holding the basket, and the feet
feeling blindly for the unreliable old steps.
Enormously sad, this unwanted quiet's suffused
with it, not the quietude you've surely yearned for,
not a solitude elected, the cell with favorite books,
savory meals left at the door, occasional nocturnal
visits (but that would compromise the solitude,
wouldn't it?) *Sad, so sad*—compared to *what?*
To your earlier more oblivious state?
It never was oblivious enough—
always those presentiments of sadness
prickling the limbic. Now a voice says, *Get outside
yourself, go walk on the flats. The tide's gone out*—
but your little metal detector will detect little metallic coins
of enormous sadness in the teeming wet sand,
and then, the tide will come back, erasing, cleansing!
And you, standing there in the salty scouring air—
will you still be *enormously sad,*

while the other world, outside your tiny purview, struck
by iron, reels? World of intentional iron, pure savage
organized iron of the world, it hasn't the time
that you have for your puny enormous sadness.

Blue Umbrella

Deer Isle

Kai says, "Here, let me fix that, you don't know
how." This elegant mechanism, a present
from my daughter, topped by its own wind hat,
engineered not to turn inside out in nor'easters
or August hurricanes. Ingenious invention of China
and Egypt, emblem of rank in remote antiquity,
collapsible shade, pampering portable sunscreen
at least a millennium before a damp Brit eureka'd
the thought of keeping dry. Bishop's Crusoe
fashioned one on his desolate island, had "such a time"
remembering the way the ribs would go.
Palpable perfection centuries in the making.
Cobalt canopy I left sprung open to dry outdoors,
away from the library's waxed floors. A courtesy,
I thought, and someone's shoved it into a railing,
so one of the little wooden caps that tip the steel ribs
and hold the water-proofed cloth taut, has split.
Now there's a gap in my assurance of shelter.
Ruined, ruined, I think—my small losses
resound in me today as titanic griefs—but Kai—
who makes his art from what you might call nothing—
toothpicks, mussel shells, buttons, discarded books,

garlic stems—who'll find anywhere, in Toronto
or Kowloon or at this island's dump swap shop,
the raw ingredients of his dreamy constructions,
Kai, who knows I'm not "skillful with my hands"
yet hasn't turned from me, Kai, smiling
in his yellow silk quilted jacket, in his black beret
in the rain, holds out the deft hand of friendship
and takes the ultimate umbrella to his work-
bench, carving for me two perfect maple caps,
one for now, one for the future, when he knows
in his heart I'll need another (don't things
always break?)—And won't we two be far apart?

American Ghazal

Sometimes a shift in tone is all you'd need to make you happy.
A shade, a shadow—but then you wonder, is *this* happiness?

Heady scented air of wisteria, lilacs, and vibernum
that could drown you through the seven windows.

When you lived on a peninsula, a disoriented shark stranded
in the shallows; you observed her with terror, pity, and pleasure.

May, so ruthless with your feelings: you're fiercely in love
with your two children a tumultuous continent away.

Still, you could swim naked beneath the Pleiades at high tide
and dance barefoot without music, without a partner.

Altruistic surrender—the merciful self-exoneration
of maternal memory—undone by a child's mythologies . . .

You attached a screen door to the children's room;
a determined cat could climb and cling and never reach their cribs.

Although you have not been granted all you craved, you feel
no grievance, only an abandoned nestling's agitation.

If an era ends, who will interpret the last chimes?
A café closes, currency burns. The present's an archive.

Word arrives of Tokyo's crows pecking at schoolchildren,
the elemental smear and grime in immaculate narrow alleys.

The Gemara tells us *Thou shalt observe* and *Thou shalt
remember* came down from heaven together. Remember?

Gail, you can't choose to run away—so, be alive to the work
in this room. Whatever else you've been hoping for.

Acadia

Gray-green morning, mossy, mottled.
The saw-whet owl has fallen silent,

though in the mind's near corner
he still calls out his hundred *too too toos*

a minute, his brassy *tours de force*—
tiny Acadian owl, has he abandoned

the scornful love he sought all night,
foregone the blizzard of brown feathers

romance occasions? The morning bell rings
in a dream's capricious turns—a gilt canoe,

the tilting river, cobalt trees, delicious
passion, acrobatic—but the sweet end

never reached, like Blake's ungratified desire.
A little coppery squirrel clucks and chuckles

to itself as the island wakes. Twigsong,
birdsong, chittering creatures—is this

what you think peace is, flight to where
no fear of losing love has left a scar?

A miniscule sliver of light slices
the rough cabin floor, new pale ferns uncurl—

the day's first question marks—
innocent, insistent at your half-open door.

At First, They

At first, they leaned toward me at the bassinet,

we wheeled together to the river:
in the spring, forsythia, daffodils;

then it was very cold, ice.
Hard. Slippery. That was the world—

the yellow room—Longfellow Road
("cul de sac," they called it)—

the carriage—pebbles—insects—
sycamores—river—sky.

Them.

Now they're gone, and the world—
there are darker things,

there *were* darker things
they didn't know yet; now they're gone,

it's me filling with *their* fractures, *their* artifacts:

her tenderly refinished chairs,
his "corny" jokes, her father's cracked

leather tefillin in a blue velvet bag
hidden under the stairs;

relentless inaccurate memories of a shtetl called *Chagrin;*

the fiery white of her rage, inextinguishable,
smoldering in me to despair.

Despair the landscape of our waking dream now,
the old time closed above us like a trap door.

Still, the gristle of his hope,
part of me—*me,*

the way my "wild" hair fell in my eyes.
The injured click of his "trick knee" on the stairs.

Queenie

What was a horse but a colossal
machine that sped away with me, so
finally I hung by one foot from one
stirrup and bounced along the gravel?

I'd thought I knew to make her canter
but I was dragged and scraped over
the country road, not thinking, feeling
This is It, nothing ahead for me but hurt

and blood and ugliness—Who was that
Queenie, graceful chestnut giantess,
retiree from a circus, rescued
from the glue factory or saved from

being horsemeat by the kindly father
of my friend Janet, what deliverer
of knowledge, that she—so soulful when
her huge teeth snarked an apple from my hand—

could, in one instant, catapult me,
a dauntless child of ten, from that morning
to this day I steer our car across a bridge
to your hospital and no brilliant doctor

needs to tell me what comes with the terrain,
to tell me there'll be no one to carry me
toward the stable or bring me safely home,
this day of brutal, foretold expectation.

Dana Street, December

As if I had no language
and would begin again
in the linguistics
of infancy,
but amnesiac
therefore with nothing
to say—

(unlike the woman in rehab
who could walk
and walked the linoleum
at all hours, shouting
to no one, I KNOW
THE WORDS! I KNOW THE WORDS!

—all the words
she knew)

I walked,
past a yard
overgrown, scraggly
after the first frost,
a rose—the bitterest orange—
still blooming, piercing
the morning

(My work had stopped,
I thought
forever)

—perfection
or imperfection
not the issue, a radiance
utterly itself,
pale petals tinged
fiery (provident neighbor,
astute, to nurture
that gift)

(I didn't take it)

Not to be thinking
Is this enough, this
moment, the chilled
unpromising air,
not to be wanting more
than I'd been given,
but remembering

last October when
I carried a glass vase,
its rose
lush, creamy,
across my living room
for your appreciations,

how you rose from
the rush-seated chair
to meet it, saying,

"Oh no, Gail,
the *rose* doesn't come
to you—
you go
to the rose."

The Swamp Trail

On the sand beyond the privet hedge and the sea grass and the wild roses
the sound of young men laughing, giddy girlish shrieking at the wet cold
bite of the bay. August, my white desk so near the high window, labor

and play held separate by the panes, the sea grass, the prickly hedge.
Another summer's ritual tasks not done, or undone, while the street's
gardens shifted from galas to graves—only a few leggy cosmos, and the timid,

almost hidden, anemones. Everything else bolted, dried, clipped. But
late summer's dissolve isn't my concern; no, today, it's the swamp
I pulled my brother from—the swamp trail, just after the War, forbidden

forest route to school, old pin oak and red maple, my big brother's
waterlogged leather shoes, his mud-soaked corduroys we feared the principal
would smell and tell on, though she never seemed to notice, so

when we came home the proper way, on sidewalks, Mother didn't know.
Even then, Jonny and I were growing apart, or just going silent:
we never talked about that morning. Does the swamp, the swamp trail

ever haunt him, too—or is it only me, the thrilled collaborator,
guilty, unpunished, heroic sneak? Did I really rescue him?
What *is* the task not done? The trail—is that *it?* Where follow it?

and how? Doesn't it always end in the same place, right behind
the lonely green Lyons playground with two boggy children,
before they'd ever heard of sex or homework, peering unnoticed

from behind rough trees, the dark primordial forest? We are done
with the work of childhood, it's over now, isn't it, as so much else is
finished—but still, I tell myself that Hillel says those who do not grow

grow smaller; rebuke myself, at once teacher and underachieving pupil.
An hour ago, I watched an ambulance outside my door, my neighbor's
houseguest taken ill, I saw an old man's fresh white sneakers,

his pale veiny legs, his faded shorts, being slid gently on a gurney
into the truck's hold. I'm thankful I couldn't see a terrified face or hear
the paramedics' reassuring smooth proficiencies. I want to be through

with the unanswered needs of everyone but my darling whose body's
been whacked by pain, by transmogrifying drugs. Have I misremembered
that once I could save someone, and *did,* that—braced on a rotting log

in no man's land—it wasn't hard to tug my skinny brother by the hand
out of the muck of dead bottom leaves, the decaying flesh of skunk cabbage,
out of the rich nutrient ooze, and back up onto our shadowy path?

Now:

There's no way to say it except the blunt way:
facts, searing the eye, facts in the nostrils:
what you love most becomes what

won't keep, that's the oldest part
of the story, not hard: these words slide
easily from fingertips daubing the keys:

what you learned today you learned also
long ago, and in another, more hopeful life:
no place now in the world—no matter how you say it—

untainted, or if you don't say anything,
or if you say the mornings are still
beautiful, late April's aroma of damp soil,

your neighbor's hyacinth easterish, painterly—
wouldn't that also be fact, be true?
A poet yesterday said: only poetry speaks the truth,

I knew that to be false: her gorgeous lines
breathless, staggered, obscure: if that's true,
really, then anything's true: but this report

on my desk, like a script on a stage, is fact, blunt:
which of our weapons are leaking uranium
everywhere on earth, into the nostrils,

inexorably, the pores, the eyes: how deaths
will come here and on distant deserts
and ancient cities and be reported falsely,

the young reporter's cerebral hemorrhage
not a vascular event, but uranium, too,
and those bodies in robes, "ours"

"their" bodies whose faces tried to be masked, bodies
fallen along the dunes, the roads, not:
this is fact: not someone else's, some enemy's

some *other's* fault: there are facts
undeliverable delivered from the imagination
to the page, the page, the page

from this imagination which is true
only to itself, selfish, bent
on its own peculiar and shapely truth:

The Mission

Soot everywhere. Trains, as if World War Two were our era,
pulling out of old South Station. At every grimy window,
two or three men—their postures grief-struck, heroic.

The iron terminal all my grandparents had arrived at,
their valises and sacks abulge with whatever mean
possessions they'd thought to lug into their futures.

Now I had their copper pans, their Sabbath candlesticks.
Gloom saturated the enormous room—no light motes,
no cappuccinos, no *New York Times* bestsellers. No matter

what the mission, you'd be too proud to fail to carry through. . . .
The hanging clock's hands could hardly bear the inching weight
of time; I couldn't see the arrows move, but if even one local clock

were taken for repair or replacement, we'd be saved from separation.
Were we—was I—certain you had no rational choice but to report
for duty? You shouldered an Italian leather case I'd never seen,

I, who'd polished and folded all your belongings. I touched your face,
you, already distant, aching to "get on with it," and I—I knew
a great hole was being torn in my life, my life that felt like

the kind of rice paper Japanese printmakers always seemed to use—
such colors, such defined images of comfort and beauty ripped away.
Who'd ordered you to go, to cross three continents

and three oceans, knowing the inescapable dangers? Was it
the Secretary of War, that garrulous fool? What could I have thought
to do or say to keep you from the mysterious assignment you welcomed,

impelled as you seemed to be by your headstrong restlessness,
your admirable infuriating insistence on doing what's too hard?
Was it too late? On Track Ten, obstinate, oblivious of your wife

in the metallic din, were you off to rescue, or murder,
a harmless sinner, were you already doomed to end in a dark alley,
iron and soot, by good angels untenanted? *Don't go   don't go   don't go*

Cape Air

Unserious, this zany 10-seat Cessna,
bright blue cartoon waves painted on both wings,
Eugene O'Neill's brooding face darkening
one side of the silvered body—he's gaunt,
grey, reading "Bound East for Cardiff"
as he first read it on Commercial Street, 1914,
across from the little house I live in now,
the Provincetown Players encircling him,
one of his early hungry handsome winters
at land's end before fame failed to ease
his famous torment.

           On the plane's other side,
clumsy, rolling, roiling, misshapen dunes
and a lean curvaceous vermilion version
of our Sienese stone tower dedicated
to the Pilgrims by Teddy Roosevelt
just when the town's whaling and fishing
heydays were about to become history.
The air's a damp blue-white fleece blanket
we motor laboriously through, chugging low
over the ebullient bay.

           Inches from me,
the pilot's conversational, only a boy:
"We'll lose about ten minutes, folks,

the air we're flying through's like chowder,"
(it's usually a twenty-minute flight).
The best way out is always through. . . .
New England chowder, thick with potatoes,
creamy, might just hold us up, aloft—
but sounds more like hot stew this little craft
will choke and drown in, downing five
incredulous reckless lives. Hard not to be afraid,
"flying blind." When I picture, milkily,

Boston's ballparks and parishes, fear blows
me backwards to 1968, a July night:
Jackie Washington in steamy Fenway Park,
just off a turbulent flight, tells the roaring
Gene McCarthy crowd—he was the quixotic
campaign's warm-up act—how scared he was:
I can swim a little, but I can't fly worth a damn!
A car backfires and the crowd falls silent.
McCarthy, standing on the pitcher's mound,
elevated, elegant, unscarred, an elusory hope
I never could pin my wounded faith on.
One night along the continuum of assassinations.

Cemetery Road

A claw, she called it—
her left thumb clamped
inside four clenched fingers,
she'd shriek when the doctor
pried them open. More
like an injured paw,

contracted into itself,
immovable. I'd wheel her in,
wanting someone to do
something. She wanted no more
of those invasions—she was right-
handed, she'd make do,

like the three-legged dog
trotting around the turn

of Cemetery Road yesterday,
loving its sturdy dog life—
it probably still chases
low-flying kites. No more
of those appointments,
no more doctors swarming

around her chair. *That hand's*
gone, she said, twice.

For her, to want her health back
would have been to suffer
(*not to want, the Buddha's recipe*
for the blessed absence of pain.)

Absence of pain—she didn't
want that either. . . .

Night Visitation

What *are* you in the enlarging dark—
subject that chooses me—
my dream dragon—

I think by day you're the blue
dragonfly, a *darning needle,*
stingless,

harmless, your fierce wings trans-
parent, your tiny square head
only engaged

in eating's nervy mechanics—
or is it bobbing in dread
of me?

In what dimension do you light
on my new yellow lily?
Over what

deep lakes have you deigned to float?
Are my yard's mosquitoes
delicacies

for you, rare ambrosial delights?—
or is it for *me* you track
their humming's

bloody, hazy, unwholesome
dirge? Oh, mother,
can that be you—

September

Let those who stay continue their vigil
over the terns and gulls, let them wait
for black ducks and the great blue heron
who'll come back to settle the wintry waters
of the bay whether we come or go,

I'll go now

while Stanley's Japanese anemone blooms,
so low I kneel to view its mother-of-pearl petals
ornamenting my shade two miles from the mother
plant wavering on the terraced dune,
breezy, near the blue bellflower

and the last daylilies,

my old friend nudging a new stanza,
another late season of color from the sand
he wrote the first draft of his tiered garden on
forty years ago, and revises with obstinate joy
even now,

a car and Sherb, his driver, standing by the gate.

Black Ducks

Bare vines cling to the windows, winter's calligraphy
casting abstract verse on the sunny floor

until clouds eclipse my conceit—a narrative's fleeting
chinoiserie. Eye, and mind's eye,

want to restore something that's been erased,
never to be retold. This afternoon,

I watch five black ducks huddle on the icy bay—
sweet surface feeders, what nourishment

can they find here? Cartoons, five inky strokes,
a flock, a hardy clan

of year-rounders I'll see come spring, they don't
study snow swirls as I do now for—

for what—guides to my life? How, I wonder,
do they survive, why don't they leave

together, go south? I say, too late, what you wanted
me to say: I miss you.

At my back, Commercial Street's closed shops,
its low white houses blur and disappear.

Snow has filled the doorways with rice. . . .

A Small Door

Travel—a small door to the future,
door I've dragged the past,

its weights and measures, through.
That was another century—

now the contrarian I traveled with
(my friend who could have argued

with the Guilin mountains
or engaged Xian's unearthed

terra cotta soldiers
still scanning the distance

for their dead emperor's enemies,
if he'd been able to

descend, to see
the terra cotta of their eyes)—

wakes from his morphined coma
to tell the transformed room

what an *amazing* life he's had,
he can't believe how *amazing!*

stunning us with his valediction.
(The Persian proverb says,

Write kindness in marble,
write injuries in dust.)

—And me, thinking only,
Doesn't what happens to the body

clip the spirit, too?
Then he sits up, sips a coke,

and visits. His life, I think,
clear, shapely, ended

in death's hospitable loggia,
as if the life of argument,

the *quarrel,*
had really been the form,

the path,
the reconciliation.

To Whoever May Be Concerned:

Please accept my resignation
and begin your search for my replacement.

I'm leaving the work unfinished,
not out of laziness, but a disorder

no one has diagnosed. I should have given
more warning—yet who would I have warned?

Also, I intended to be more helpful,
more encouraging, to offer advice,

some words of wisdom, but I've always
procrastinated—please forgive me.

What can I accomplish before I leave?
I meant to study cosmology. To relish

the graceful little boats in the harbor.
To hear the night music of the surf,

not think of it as black waves smacking
the seawall of my softening home.

To try to understand the body's tango,
its wishful leaps and entanglements.

Above all, I planned to write a poem
so subversive it would have exploded

secrets, articulated terror and pain,
married acceptance to paradox.

My reader would have wept and laughed
and leapt, uplifted and brilliant,

back into life. So much for intentions.
You'll find a thousand drafts locked

in my files. I've taped the key
to the underside of the keyboard.

The work is yours now. I hope
you can make something come of it.

I didn't know how.
Yours,

(suggested by Primo Levi's "Le pratiche inevase")

Rudy's Tree

Rudy Burckhardt, 1914–1999

I admire the way he took
   matter into his own hands,
     (he didn't bring his camera

this summer—and when his son
   brought it from the city,
     never loaded it), carried

his wooden easel in from
   its station in the woods,
     the night before, no film

in his old camera, free
   of desire, the calm I imagine
     he carried with him

into the cool water,
   the early morning resolve,
     his long life behind him,

autonomous, various,
   the pond familiar,
     and dark. And now, I look into

the furrows of his painting
    hanging on my sunlit stair-
        wall in Provincetown,

the ridged bark, the deep
    fissures, gray, brown,
        black: a tree all trunk,

tree I can imagine him
    conversing with, around them
        slender new trees, green

summer ferns, a fallen pine,
    twigs, the tender lyric line
        of one luminous white

birch in the still Maine woods.
    A quiet conversation—
        like ours when we spoke

only days ago. Is it a pine?
    A hemlock? The bark
        is rough, articulate,

dense, a texture craggy
    with age. At the picture's
        heart, an inner layer, glowing.

Did I tell him that day
    how much I love living
        with it?

To X

Angst, you'd call it,
ennui and angst—
and you haven't called
or written, or done anything
to help my ugly mood. Is your heart
a fist of marble? I'm hurt,
but it's good you've ignored me,
your friendship's no cure-all.
—Oh, but a word from you
might have fixed everything,
though more full of recrimination
than a soliloquy of Lear's!

—after Catullus

Seven Sons

You knew the Founding Fathers, all five
Great Lakes, every capitol of every state.
When the teacher asked her questions
you always raised your hand, you thought
her whole momentous enterprise might be
an embarrassed failure without you.

You read a book a day, hard ones:
gold stars gleamed beside your name,
a glittering, prideful dance along
one line of Miss Tate's book-report
chart. Those stars always in mind,
you read in the kitchen, the cloakroom,

even on the tarmac at noon recess.
Breakfast, dinner, tag, kickball—
you'd be reading something. Saturdays,
your father drove from Auburndale
to Brookline, to Temple Israel.
You learned the Hebrew alphabet,

the dietary laws, a lot of psalms
and the begats. Sundays, the other
Burr School kids would walk to church,
to Corpus Christi or the "First Congo";

Wednesdays, to Junior Fellowship.
Some of them, not many, were children

of missionaries. They all lived
in the Missionary Home on the hill—
dilapidated, different but not exactly
foreign. Old people rocked in gliders
on a wraparound front porch.
They'd usually stay a year or two

(you never were invited in),
then back to India or Africa or China.
One of your grandfathers was born
in America, the other was a blacksmith
in the Old Country. No one you knew
had died. You had to know everything:

how a scab forms; the causes
of the Revolution; what *amber waves
of grain* were; what sins Catholics cleansed
when they made Confession; the reason
Hannah let her seven sons be torn
limb from limb then roasted on a rack

rather than partake of "swine's flesh,"
rather than forsake the dietary laws—
why didn't she just tell them *Ess!*
the way your grandmother told you?
Weren't they terrified of pain? How could
they face the dreadful punishment?

Why did Antiochus the Babylonian
king slaughter her boys one by one

for not eating pork? Why not eat a *little?*
Was there a difference between "good" and "evil"?
What made her a heroine for teaching those refusals?
Who could you ask? The rabbi said

someday you'd know. Know *what?*
What change could occur within you
so you'd understand the history of the Jews?
What *were* children to the king? To the mother?
Who could explain the question inside
your question? If Hannah and her sons

were right, weren't they also God-forsaken?
What mattered to them more than *life?*
The dinner table had no place for this discussion.
The questions tossed your bed at night;
you'd only wake with more; they multiplied
like the little boy's hats in your sister's book

that reproduced on his sinless head,
each one more extravagantly lavish,
more intricate and unwanted than the last,
no matter how fast he tried to doff them
to the tyrannical king demanding he bow
bareheaded, subservient, like all the other subjects.

Waterlilies

They were children at a party. The lights
were out, someone's parents upstairs watching
situation comedies. What was the music playing
on the phonograph? What were the children's
names? Were the girls laughing, and the boys?

—*Dance* music, it was music to dance close
to, the basement door was closed, the 6 boys
and the 6 girls were clumsy, ardent
in the dazzling darkness. It was spring,
early June, I think, yes, the magnolia

was blown, and on the river, the large green
shield-like lily pads curled a little, the showy
fragrant blooms of the waterlilies closed
for the night. The luscious white petals, closed.
Where did they begin, the tangling roots—

in the mud at the bottom? The girl knew which boy
she wanted to dance with. That afternoon,
his hand had brushed hers—on purpose?—
when they'd picked up their spelling tests
at the teacher's desk. 100 percent for her;

for him, as usual, 50. He couldn't spell
"balloon" or "cinnamon," but his body's

genius was sparkling, she'd touched it once
at Miss Boudreau's desk. In the dark,
in her fearless body, she danced something

like a waltz from dance class. Her body,
poor pleasured thing, didn't know
what it meant, coming to life as it did,
so precipitously, all its parts fitting,
forsaking its sappy past. The next day,

she and a boy would take a rowboat
out onto a jungle of waterlilies impossible
to pick, their long rubbery stems invisible,
never-ending. On the bank, weeping willow,
wild garlic. The oars, heavy wooden oars.

A Saturday. That was it: one warm inaugural
night's swaying, then the sun's insinuations,
the carnal tugging at fathomless blossoms.
One day only, one day in the epochal romance
of the Charles River, one day of being with.

His hair was yellow, his face the beautiful
impassive face of a Greek god she'd seen
in the Book of Knowledge, perfect, sightless,
and after that, she wanted only to be alone,
she wanted only not to be alone.

Zeppo's First Wife

"One of Doc's cousins married one of those 5 brothers, the funny ones, who
were they?"
"The Marx brothers?"
"Yes, them, the youngest, I don't remember the name—"
"Zeppo."
"Yes, Zeppo. They got divorced."
—A late conversation with my mother

"Why should I care about posterity? What's posterity ever done for me?"
—Groucho Marx

He married a cousin, or actually, my grandfather's
half brothers' cousin. No one here remembers
Zeppo's first wife, related to my great half uncles
Phil and Jesse, high-living lawyers in New York,
"bachelor brothers," a little unsavory—

they dated showgirls; when Jesse invested
in a Broadway play, he whispered to me
he owned "a piece of *Fanny!*" Their father,
Simon, my great-grandfather, owned a haberdashery
in Rockland, Maine. *Whose* cousin was it

married Zeppo, the blank, born Herbert, smarmy
amidst his dervish brothers, the baby whose mother

put him in the act when Gummo joined the army?
Bystander at his brothers' rioting subversions—
their chaos in a cauldron—the ingénue,

the "romantic lead," never one of the brilliant
enfants terribles. Straight man, no puns,
no double entendres, more victim than Marxian
tormentor. (People who really knew them
said he was the funniest.) But once, on tour

in Omaha, when Groucho had appendicitis,
Zeppo painted the greasepaint mustache
above his lip, roughed up his slick black hair,
donned black-rimmed glasses, and brought the house
down. The audience never knew—*no one* knew

Zeppo could be as unzipped as his zany
unloved older brother. (Was that his zenith
or his nadir?) He never had that chance again—
"*He was so good,*" Groucho was known
to say, "*it made me get better quicker!*"

—Groucho with his zero-sum philosophy:
a win for anyone could only be a cataclysmic
loss for him. So, in the end, Adolph the angelic
demon harpist, Leonard the gambler,
and T. S. Eliot's pen pal, Julius, Groucho

kept the act alive, leering into unfunny age,
with a callow crooner always filling the fourth
pair of shoes. And Zeppo? He was an inventor,
he created a clamping device our Air Force used
in the atomic raid on Hiroshima, then he teamed

with Gummo, real Americans reinventing
themselves, two also-rans, they partnered up,
began a talent agency and thrived.
And the first wife? my state-of-Maine twice
unremembered distant half cousin nonce removed

whose name I find this morning on the web,
Marion Benda—footnote to a footnote—she's gone,
of course, as the brothers are, through the zodiacal lights
beyond stardom and failure, beyond his family's
history and ours of raves and flops. Replaced,

forgotten. Not missed. *Only the hand that touched
the hand,* my mother would say dismissively,
but surely something more, something happier.
Her life not so unlike yours or mine, or Zeppo's,
then: he never got top billing, no one's idea

of the zeitgeist of the Jazz Age—except that night
his brother's biographer uncovered: he came in
first, he was the rage, he lived in an audience's
delirious laughter, lived, not quite himself,
in the roar of its applause. And then, he left the stage.

They Can't Take That Away from Me (2001)

Five Poems Entitled "Questions"

QUESTIONS

What is my purpose in life
if not to peer into the glazed bowl
of silence and fill it for myself
with words? How shall I do it?
The way a disobedient child sings
to herself to keep out the punishing
night, not knowing that her brother
and sister, hearing the song,
shift in their cots of demons
and are solaced into sleep?

QUESTIONS

What is my purpose in life
if not to feed myself
with vegetables and herbs
and climb a step machine to nowhere
and breathe deeply to calm myself
and avoid loud noises
and the simmering noon sun?
Isn't there more,
more even than turning to you,
remembering what drew us together,

wondering what will tear us apart?
Does it matter if I tell
my one story again and then again,
changing only a tracing of light,
a bit of fabric, a fragment of
laughter, a closed cafeteria—
if I add a detail almost every day
of my life, what will I have done?
Who will I give my collections to,
who would want to use them?
Don't answer, don't make me
hang my head
in gratitude or shame.

QUESTIONS

What is my purpose in life
if not, when there is nothing to say,
to control myself and say nothing?

What could wisdom be if not
a mastery of waiting and listening?
Is it my purpose to become wise?

What is wisdom? Isn't it a pose,
the will refusing realms of confusion?
How would I approach it, unless

I learned to love the absence of speech,
even the implication of language,
so violently I'd remind myself

of a friend who detests the mimes
who gesticulate on Sundays in the park,
and has begun a postcard campaign

to Silence the Silent. She knows
gestures, too, are a part of speech.
Would it have enough meaning for me,

to watch and listen, to touch
the warm fur of animals and the sandy dunes,
to drop handfuls of fine gravel

into the graves of the newly dead,
to learn grief from the mourner's tears
and courage from their squared shoulders

as they return, each one alone
to the limousines? What gives anyone
the daring to adore paradoxical life?

Won't I always yearn for and fear an answer?
Will I someday have the one thing to say
that contradicts and clarifies itself,

and without falseness or sorrow,
without strutting or stumbling,
will I know to say it?

QUESTIONS

What is my purpose in life
if not to practice goodness

I know isn't graphed in my genes
the way designs are programmed
in the cells of a butterfly's wing?
How can I pretend
that the modest beauty of self-
lessness is not a false glory?
Why hope altruism is part of me,
set into the elegant machinery
by which form and temperament
are generated? The saints are boring
and fictional, their great acts
accidents of a moment, reactions
to cataclysm. What is goodness?
Haven't I tried long enough,
stepped on my own heart, broken
my hands trying to pry it open?
Haven't I lain awake, my head
aching with the chronic dementia
of the would-be virtuous? Haven't I
settled on my right to be harmless,
nothing better? Didn't I fail
at sacrificing, wasn't the last time
it worked when my son and daughter
still slept in their own messy beds?
Who did they think mothered them,
without rage or tears, with no ideas
of escape? Now they are thrilling
voices on the phone, they're at home
in the world, they have discrete selves,
there are layers to them, they are like
poems. What will I do from sunrise
to midnight now they don't use me,
why should I take on anyone's pain?

How will I live if I won't care
for anything in this world again
more than I care for myself?

QUESTIONS

What is my purpose in life
now that it's too late for regret,

now that I've apologized
to the murdered dead and the ones

who went with tubes & needles
on ungiving rubberized beds

and the ones who left glowing,
lovers holding their thin cold hands,

compassionate angels hovering
in the sweetish light of candles,

snow folding itself gently outside
over the dry summer gardens,

soothing the streetlights
and the angular cars, and hydrants?

What can I want now but to be
solitary in a white cell,

with only a mattress and table,
my soul simplifying as Thoreau

advised? I know I'll want one thing
on my wall, a framed poem of Li Po's,

the Chinese characters say the moon
is making him homesick, drunk and lonely,

I'll want 5 things on my table:
a block of woven paper; a brush;

a stone brushrest in the shape
of the 4 sacred mountains;

I'll want to look at a Chinese rock,
small and violent like my soul,

mountainous as the landscape
of Guilin, vertical *jade hairpins;*

and then, a gold and red pagoda,
a ceramic music box—

when I wind a key, it will play
a folk song I've heard only once

on ancient instruments years ago
as I sat on a carved bench

watching huge golden carp
swimming madly in the miniature lake

of a scholar's garden in Suzhou;
it will play in perfect time

for a while until it winds slowly
down, and then the dying song

will pull me mercifully back
to my calm, impenitent room.

II

Maybe It's Only the Monotony

of these long scorching days
but today my daughter
is truly exasperating—
Stop it! I shout—*or I'll*—
and I twist her little pinked arm
slowly,
calibrating my ferocity—

You can't hurt me you can't hurt me!
She's so defiant, glowering,
glaring at me—
but frightened,
her eyes bright with tears—
See, I'm not even crying!

I see. But it's the angel
of extermination
I see, shining
in his black trappings,
and turning ecstatically
toward him, a little Jewish girl
tempts him
to play his game of massacre.

—after Vittorio Sereni

Not Crying

Whatever the intention,
a poem about grief is not grief,
nor the expression or cry of it.
So, if I describe a Jewish cemetery,
the small gray or brown pebbles
on the broad sill of a gravestone
("What does that mean?" my daughter
asks at my father's grave.
"Kilroy was here!"
my stoical mother answers,
embarrassed as she is
by an Old Country tradition
which I explained to her
last time, the pebble that says
"I was here," or "always."
Dry-eyed mother, one moment
irreverent and the next,
sentimentalizing father's
perfections—a far cry
from the litany of complaint
still lingering in my phone's
limbic); or if I should describe
my tears as I stood there
with Kathe, nine years after
his unveiling, that would be
description—not crying.

My young cousin ill
at our aunt's open grave
the next row of stones over,
a chiselled row of names
from my childhood my children
will never know. This is paper,
ink, not a heart breaking
—nor a healing, either.
Something I make,
so when the day is over
there's something here.

Evening

Sometimes she's Confucian—
resolute in privation. . . .

Each day, more immobile,
hip not mending, legs swollen;

still she carries her grief
with a hard steadiness.

Twelve years uncompanioned,
there's no point longing for

what can't return. This morning,
she tells me, she found a robin

hunched in the damp dirt
by the blossoming white azalea.

Still there at noon—
she went out in the yard

with her 4-pronged metal cane—
it appeared to be dying.

Tonight, when she looked again,
the bird had disappeared and

in its place, under the bush,
was a tiny egg—

"Beautiful robin's-egg blue"—
she carried carefully indoors.

"Are you keeping it warm?"
I ask—what am I thinking?—

And she: "Gail, I don't want
a *bird,* I want a blue egg."

I Wish   I Want   I Need

The black kitten cries at her bowl
meek meek and the gray one glowers
from the windowsill. My hand on the can
to serve them. First day of spring.
Yesterday I drove my little mother for hours
through wet snow. Her eightieth birthday.
What she wanted was that ride with me—
shopping, gossiping, mulling old grievances,
1930, 1958, 1970.
How cruel the world has been to her,
how uncanny she's survived it.
In her bag, a birthday card
from "my Nemesis," signed *Sincerely
with love*—"Why is she doing this to me?"
she demands, "She *hates* me."
                              "Maybe
she loves you" is and isn't what Mother
wants to hear, maybe after sixty years
the connection might as well be love.
Might well be love, I don't say—
I won't spoil her birthday,
my implacable mother.
                    In Byfield,
in the snowstorm, we bought things
at an antiques mall, she a miniature
Sunbonnet Baby creamer and saucer—

a bargain!—I, a chrome ice bucket
stamped with penguins, with Bakelite handles.
I wanted it, I had one just like it
at home. Sometimes I think the only thing
I'm sure I want is what I have.

"What do you wish for?" I asked
a friend, I was so curious to know
how he'd formulate a wish, to know
if there *is* a formula. His list
was deliciously simple, my friend
the hedonist: a penthouse with a concierge,
"wonderful food," months in Mexico,
good movies. . . .

                    Last night, you and I
watched "The Way We Were" and I cried—
I always do—for the wanting in it,
and the losing. "It's a great movie,"
I said, to justify my tears. I wish
you were more like me. Streisand and Redford,
so opposite it's emblematic, almost
a cliché. Each wants or needs the other
to change, so the pushy Jewish lefty,
Barbara, should be quiet, accommodating,
and the accommodating, handsome, laid-back
"nice gentile boy" should agree with her
that people *are* their principles.
He thinks people can relax a little,
be happy. If only
                    they could both become
nothing, they can stay together.
All her wishing and wanting and needing

won't make that happen. She marches
against the Nazis, the Blacklist, the bomb,
through the movie decades, and he doesn't
want to be a great unpopular novelist,
so he writes badly for movies,
and later, television.
                    At the end
(it's the early '60s), when they meet again
in front of the Plaza, his look—the blank
Redford quizzicality I've learned
is his whole expressive repertoire—
seems to ask, "Why? Why did I love you?
Why do I still? Why aren't you
like me?"
                    And because the director's
a liberal, Streisand's the wiser one,
more human than Redford—she's leafletting,
to ban the bomb, in the '70s she'll be
Another Mother for Peace—the way
she wriggles her sensual mouth
(a mannerism that's become familiar
in the years since this movie was new)
I know she loves him or at least yearns
for him, still wants him, which is more
piercing, more *selfish*.
                    This morning, my throat
is constricted, my head aches, I'm always
like this, this movie reminds me you don't get
what you want, even if you're not weak,
or mean, or criminal. I wish I didn't
believe that message so utterly. Today
I need to believe something more useful,
more positive.

Once, when I was a child,
my mother lied to me. Maybe that day
I was too demanding, more likely I needed
consolation—my schoolmates so lucky,
so confident, so gentile. Either
she meant to reassure me, or—more likely—
to instruct when she said (she couldn't have
believed it, the '40s had happened)
that the meek inherit the earth. That was
lesson one of our course in resignation.
My little mother,
                          little kitten,
be patient, I'm trying, it's for you
I'm opening this can of worms,
for you I'm opening this can of food.

Young Apple Tree, December

What you want for it what you'd want
for a child: that she take hold;
that her roots find home in stony

winter soil; that she take seasons
in stride, seasons that shape and
reshape her; that like a dancer's,

her limbs grow pliant, graceful
and surprising; that she know,
in her branchings, to seek balance;

that she know when to flower, when
to wait for the returns; that she turn
to a giving sun; that she know to share

fruit as it ripens, that what's lost
to her will be replaced; that early
summer afternoons, a full blossoming

tree, she cast lacy shadows; that change
not frighten her, rather change
meet her embrace; that remembering

her small history, she find her place
in an orchard; that she be her own
orchard; that she outlast you;

that she prepare for the hungry world,
the fallen world, the loony world,
something shapely, useful, new, delicious.

The Weskit

Thirteen rings,
then her thready voice
apologizing:

I'm sorry I took so long to answer,
I had to drag these two big feet
from the kitchen. Well.

I dreamt about you last night —
Don't worry, nothing bad happened to you —
We were together in a cold room,

I was wearing a little weskit,
a wool vest, and I didn't want you
to be cold, so I told you, Put it on,

but you wouldn't — you said
that would make you just like me.
You said, I don't want to be like you! —

After the call, I went into the kitchen
to complain to him, to remind myself
that I only want to be harmless —

but even in *her* dreams I'm rejecting;
to confess I'm afraid
my yearning to be good is only rage

to think well of myself—
like *her* need to give, my mother
who'll stand for hours

at the shaky stove, stirring the pot:
I know you hate soup, but take this,
it's good for you —

and I accept jars afloat with barley
and shove them into the freezer,
resisting the gift I don't want

as if I won't be mothered,
as if I've always been
inconsolable. . . .

I'd been away,
I *hadn't* phoned until morning.
Now, that small purchase of time

seemed heartless—Now,
I felt I should apologize
for *her* dream . . .

Then, as he half-listened, patient
and bored, re-folding the *Times,*
I suddenly saw her dream differently,

as if it were not about my rejecting her
nor about her manipulating me
in the re-telling:

Mother, I thought, you must not want me
to shiver, as you do in the chill
of widowhood.

You reach to cover me
in your dream, but I shout
NO! I don't want it!

I'm afraid to be like you!
I refuse to live in your loneliness,
your bitter spleen!

I stood in the stunned morning light
at our round oak table,
feeling for a moment the remorse

and satiety of one who *is* loved.
I granted my mother her tenderness . . .
But then I thought,

Who is the *author* of this dream?
Must I enter her and
invent her maternal compassion?

or—as I've always feared,
furious with her determinacy—
is she still *in me,*

omniscient mother, mother
with "eyes in the back of her head,"
mother from whom there are no secrets—

not even my fears, not even in sleep;
mother dreaming my dreams for me,
speaking in the old tone

of accusation, tone of sorrow,
of irreducible pain, speaking
my own private night language. . . .

Whatever the significance of the vest,
I could take it, couldn't I—
scratchy, smelling of mothballs,

brown with suffering, premonitory
offering I might be warmed by
if I let go, if I give in.

Narrow, color of dry oak leaves
in late November, tortoiseshell
buttons I see and feel,

why can't I accept it, slip
my arms through each armhole,
tug it across my broad shoulders?

Who else would use it?
Couldn't I pull it from back to front
even though it's tight for me,

even if the buttonholes
don't reach the round buttons—
couldn't I be grateful? Couldn't I wear it?

Penumbra

Mother of my birth, how lonely
it must be in the fierce
aftermath of will,

and how I dither, here
with my vocabulary of refusals
and longing, as if

any word might burn us.
Now I long to comfort you
and be consoled by you,

and you—
nothing softened
but the durable, unendurable

body which betrays us
all, and brings the spirit
down with it.

The burden of our memories—
what was once painful to endure—
to what purpose

should I recall them to us?
Yet they are what we have:
what you said, where

you drove me, our plunge
into the backyard river depths
where Daddy saved me—

Clever mother of my birth,
of oatmeal and x-ray vision,
of moral lessons and the world

as enemy, who waited for me
to love you,
as I couldn't help loving,

when your cracked rages
against me had no source
we could acknowledge—

now I want to tell you,
Don't speak, let me imagine
your sweetness, my soothing

devotion, not that harshness
palpable
as a stone curtain

no caress can reach through,
not to us—not to you
furious in your crank bed,

not to me, alight here
on an orange armchair,
while the television goes on and on,

loud, cacophonous,
a million gaudy circuses,
unfathomable circuitry.

Last Night

Mother, when I left you last night
in the forlorn clutter of your collections,
the May sky turning lavender, the lush magnolias
drinking the antique dusk of Commonwealth Avenue

where seventy years ago, you marched,
a small brave daughter of paranoiacs haunted
by Cossacks, your untried engine fueled,
by the blighted certainties of old Boston—

you wanted, you *loved* the deracinated manners,
the kindly condescensions, the classical
education awaiting your entrance, answers
to a child's roiling questions, child

gallantly rescued by Greek and Latin, by battles,
dates, monuments, by algebras and elegies
and sonnets—mnemonics you'll still invoke
for your trying daughter. . . . Last night,

after I'd finally fallen asleep, I hid again
in your attic, my cheek pressed to a green gown
hanging from a splintered beam. Calmed, soothed
by crushed velvet, safe among moth-eaten sweaters,

puzzles with missing pieces, Chinese Checkers,
my right hand brushed a gilt-edged book,
its binding a pale brown leather; gold lettering
tooled in the cover, *The Book of Questions.*

The Book of Questions—it brought *your* mother back,
her glass-doored cabinet, the brass key she kept hidden
until, on Saturdays, I'd beg her to take *The Book
of Knowledge* down for me. I assumed you'd found *your* key

to America there—to the Public Library, to Latin School,
to college. Grandmother would give magnanimous
permission, then perform the weekly sacrament
of unlocking. I'd turn the old-style pages, I was sure

to be filled with wisdom, or—was there a difference?—
with information. On the green sofa, her *davenport,*
in the dusty St. Paul Street Sabbath morning,
I'd touch the pictures, I'd almost touch the Wonders

of the World. I felt secure that history's riches
had been secured for *me* in the nineteenth century.
Last night, I wanted to see the Sphinx again,
the Taj Mahal, the Nile! Last night, in the warmth

of the past, in our attic, I couldn't open
the buttery cover to that tome of questions.
But what could harm me there? What moral
do I think is in it? What do I know is coming?

Is it that in the unfinished moonlit attic,
there'll be no mortal answers I can use,

only my black infinity of questions? *Mother,*
I'm afraid of grief, and I mean to enter it fully.

My Dream after Mother Breaks Her Hip

She can walk
We're in a grimy park in Guanzhou
by the White Swan Hotel

She's practicing *tai chi*
her indigo pajamas and black slippers
just like the other miniature

old women their smooth gestures
their flexibility and serenity
their healed feet tiny

as kindergarteners
and how fluid she is my smart mother
turning aside now to remind me

Gail
stand up straight the spine
is the Pillar of Heaven

But I'm worried and whiny
flailing in the shadow of a tree,
incapacitated as in life

and she turns back
to her new slow motion
Old men squat murmuring

by their confused caged birds
freed like this each morning
from unlit rooms

I can't dream her power away
I'm caught here
in eternity's shade

where I begin to move
gradually gracelessly
to embrace her

Tree   muse   emptiness
cage   world

They Can't Take That Away from Me

The way the blue car spun tonight
on imperceptible ice—that stop-
time: bare pocked sycamores, the river's
black sheen, the football stadium
empty of Romans, the oblivious sky-
line shining like a festivity—
and, shaken, I could still straighten
the formidable blue invention,
slide the delinquent wheels to a curb;

the way, in South China, the car radio
says, believers crowd closet-like shops
to purchase tiny packets of Bear Bile,
a favorite cure-all, while bears go mad
in their abscessing bodies, in cages
barely their height, hurling themselves,
banging their agonized heads at the bars—
lifetimes of pain only, for the ancient
sake of a fierce "medicinal harvest";

the way a mother stirring sweet batter
in a well-lit kitchen, feels the Pyrex
bowl slip to the floor, and it breaks,
and seeing there'll be no upside-down cake
for dinner, shrieks at her little boy
cowering in the doorway, *Look what*

you made me do! and lunges to smack him,
the way she'd struck yesterday and last week,
though he's still as a stalled truck;

the way I felt last night when she hung up
on me, I knew I had hurt her because her mind
's gone, and I refused for my life
to let mine follow again; the way I held
the dead phone, relieved to be not
listening at last—*the memory of all that,
no no*—relieved, selfish, and empty:
wouldn't I choose if I could not to be human or
any other mammal programmed for cruelty?
No, they can't take that away from me

III

Hypnosis

5th floor . . . 4th . . . 3rd . . . flickering
lit numbers above an art deco door
in the brain's elevator, a polished
marble cage dropping you smoothly
to the luxurious lobby of Serenitas
Hotel — a '30s spa, a hangout
graced by Garbo and Groucho, grège
carpet, gleaming door sliding open
toward the cabanas, the stucco arches,
a giant fig tree dappling the ceramics,
benevolent waiters posed artfully
by cool palmettos, invented only to
attend you. But you're not relaxing,
not yet. Conflict. Distraction. Close
your eyes now, recline in your webbed
reclining chair, try to imagine
imagining a magnetized barge floating
on the East River, attracting your terrors
like little iron filings zipping
headlong through air to settle on its deck
(But does a barge have a deck? where
exactly do your troubles land?) Oh,
you can let them go, they're bits of metal
dust flying elsewhere, until your eyelids
grow heavy, your chest is heaving
in an optimistic imitation of deep

breathing. But your left arm's cramping;
a dire tautness above your right ear;
your jaw's screwed tight as a dill pickle
jar. You'd better abandon that unseaworthy
scow, envision a soothing warm light
fills your veins instead, floods your limbs,
both your legs unravel, your ankles
angle helplessly toward heaven or hell,
evil exits by the ten toes, a drowsy
something as if something. . . . Now a voice
spells deliverance from your half-head
stabbed by familiars of pain, old noisemakers
of the embroidered white pillowcase,
deliverance from Mass Avenue's repertory
company of sirens, racing racing racing,
you can't silence the one who's clashing
cymbals, who's dropping syllables, who stokes
the day's rages, the one who always co-signs
your black pages — or can you? What on earth
could you be forgetting? What's happening
to your mind's habits? What hope is there
for transformation? What vigil is this
selfish exercise interrupting? What fissure —
what fraying — loosens the fabric of fear,
of perturbation? Where are you going?
or have your arrived? You know,
this is no time for these questions,
your lit feet are fluttering,
you're sinking, diving, plummeting —

At the Ear, Nose, and Throat Clinic

One of those appointments you postpone
until anxiety propels you to the phone,
then have to wait too long for, to take
an inconvenient time . . . Late in the day,
an old man and I watch the minute hand

on the waiting room wall. I've papers
to grade, but he wants someone to talk to,
and his attendant's rude, so he turns
his whiskery face to me: "Y' know, I lived
my whole life in Waltham, worked 40 years

at the watch factory—oh, that city used to be
so beautiful, now it's a mess, those Cubans
and Puerto Ricans, they ruined it."
Coiled in his wheelchair, he's mad
for company, probably scared he's dying,

*

and so am I. I don't remember Watch City
as beautiful the year I was eleven,
when Merle and I rode the Grove Street bus
to Moody Street to shoplift haircurlers
and Pond's Vanishing Cream, nickel items

at the Waltham Woolworth's. It was
an old factory town, wooden triple-deckers,
water rats swimming in the oily river.
Merle and I didn't risk a furtive life
of crime in our well-kempt Auburndale

where we thought we were well-known,
and canoers paddled the same Charles River
past our homes. And I still wonder
what could have vanished when we rubbed
the mystery elixir on our silky cheeks?

*

His cheeks sucked in, this geezer could be
my grandfather forty years ago, so
I ignore his racist overture and agree
Waltham *was* beautiful, as the attendant
takes his Social Security card,

and whistles: "Boy, are you old!"
then mutters something else in Spanish.
The number must be low. . . . "1936—
that was the first year of Social Security!"
the old guy brags. The kid forsakes

our ancient history, flexes his muscles.
He's probably been listening
to insults for an hour in the Elder Van,
he's bored and angry—why should he be
nice? Yet hungry for a distracting

fact or story, I encourage the grandfather,
I want to be treated well myself some day,
when I'll need it even more than I do now. . . .
My little bids for attention, my birds, fragile
fluttering words, desire to be visible and seen. . . .

"FDR was okay, wasn't he?" I'm playing
90, it's what I do to make us both
less lonely, reminisce as if we'd shared
the '30s, as if I'd been there, come
from Sicily or Limerick, a seamstress

earning her hard living one town over.
I always sat this way with Doc, years
after he'd retired, his best treasure
(besides my golden mother) a gold
pocket watch, a handsome Waltham watch—

*

a different time, when the things
a person held or owned weren't many
but were permanent, a part of who you were.
So his elegant watch confused me toward
the idea my little dentist grandfather

had some connection to the company,
as if he'd labored there, a master craftsman,
had been rewarded by a grateful boss.
His bit of luxury, the swirling monogram
on the back (which opened with a click),

IR, for Isaac Rosenberg, timepiece
connected by a chain to a safety pin
at his frayed striped trouser pocket;
another pin secured his Shawmut bankbook,
deposits he'd made decades before

*

that I'd inherit, $214, Shawmut branch
nearby the long-gone Waldorf Cafeteria
where he idled weekday mornings
with his cronies, also reminiscing,
I suppose (although then I didn't think

of it), the Good Old Days before
the motorcar, before their children
moved away. Dexterity and skill gone, too,
from his arthritic hands. He relished
those mornings! The black-and-white

tiled floor, the nearly empty tables,
the Perfection Salad, Welsh rarebit,
the "bloomberry pie." The counterman.
They serve an elegant porridge there,
he told me, gourmet of the ordinary,

State of Maine-ah grandfather, my *Mainiac.*
The soon-to-be-widowed wives elsewhere,
polishing mahogany veneer, or playing
bridge, or shopping Coolidge Corner
from butcher to baker in prescient

black dresses. Old men and women
so relieved to be rid of the burden
of one another for a whole morning,
of the tired bickering sentences
of long American marriages, of pain

and disappointment. What memories
they'd had of courtships long since passed on
to grandchildren, and half-false anyway,
like studio photographs, mythic stories
they could live with; now forgotten,

the mistakes they'd been too fearful
or devout to rectify. I miss that
cafeteria, the whole *idea* of cafeterias,
although Doc never took me, just pointed
to it on our Sunday drive, repeating

paeans to gray porridge, something no
description's glow could make me want.
Waltham had them, too, free-fire zones
a kid alone could enter with five cents
for huge iced cookies, black-and-whites,

*

half chocolate, half vanilla, all Crisco
and white sugar, chewed in gluttonous
companionable half-light, wonderful—
But who'd know that now? Who cares?
Merle and I did everything subversive

we could imagine—which wasn't much.
I'm sure I cruised Sin City in my mind,
decayed old town—nowhere—but to me
forbidden fruit: the 5 & 10, eyelash
curlers, odd metal torture instruments

I smuggled home that pinched my lids
and made my lashes angle wildly up,
delinquent startled in the bathroom
mirror; Tangee lipsticks the size
of my little finger, unflattering coral;

pink girdles I'd eye furtively, wondering
that I'd have to wriggle into one someday,
or wear the bony corset my grandmother
assured me was my fate. Oh, esoteric glamorous
puzzle of the vanished vanishing cream . . .

                    *

Later, not *so* much later, the first day
of my driver's license, I drove the family
station wagon down Moody Street and banged
the traffic policeman's rubber perch.
He jumped down before it bounced the street,

and yelled me over in a rage. Or maybe,
he was kindly, it's only my criminal terror
I remember, of punishment fine-tuned,
my ruined life, my new rights vanishing.
Hardly a threat, I know now, the feckless cop.

I gripped the steering wheel so hard
to stop the huge recalcitrant Ford, doomed
to lose my brand-new temporary license—
How could I think, my budding power stripped,
I'd ever get the chance to live or drive?

Girl in a Library

" . . . But my mind, gone out in tenderness,
Shrinks from its object . . . "
　　　　　　　　—Randall Jarrell

I want to find my way back to her,
to help her, to grab her hand, pull her
up from the wooden floor of the stacks
where she's reading accounts of the hatchet
murders of Lizzie Borden's harsh parents
as if she could learn something about
life if she knew all the cuts and slashes;

her essay on Wordsworth or Keats
only a knot in her belly, a faint pressure
at her temples. She's pale, it's five years
before the first migraine, but the dreamy
flush has already drained from her face.
I want to lead her out of the library,
to sit with her on a bench under a still

living elm tree, be *one who understands,*
but even today I don't understand,
I want to shake her and want to assure her,
to hold her—but love's not safe for her,

although she craves what she knows
of it, love's a snare, a closed door,
a dank cell. Maybe she should just leave

the campus, take a train to Fall River,
inspect Lizzie's room, the rigid corsets
and buttoned shoes, the horsechair sofas,
the kitchen's rank stew. Hell. Bleak
loyal judgmental journals of a next-door
neighbor—not a friend, Lizzie had no friend.
If only she could follow one trajectory

of thought, a plan, invent a journey
out of this place, a vocation—
but without me to guide her, where
would she go? And what did I ever offer,
what stiffening of spine? What goal?
Rather, stiffening of soul, her soul
cocooned in the library's trivia.

Soul circling its lessons. What can I say
before she walks like a ghost in white lace
carrying her bouquet of stephanotis,
her father beaming innocently at her side,
a boy waiting, trembling, to shape her?
He's innocent, too, we are all innocent,
even Lizzie Borden who surely did take

the axe. It was so hot that summer morning.
The hard-hearted stepmother, heavy hand
of the father. There was another daughter
they favored, and Lizzie, stewing at home,

heavy smell of mutton in the pores
of history. But this girl, her story's
still a mystery—I tell myself she's a quick

study, a survivor. There's still time.
Soon she'll close the bloody book,
slink past the lit carrels, through
the library's heavy door to the world.
Is it too late to try to touch her,
kneel beside her on the dusty floor
where we're avoiding her assignment?

Twenty Lines before Breakfast

Is it hereditary, this maundering every morning
like a hermit, hesitating by the solarium
as if a choice of Grape-nuts or dry bagel
would foredoom you? Foredoom to what,

what hemidemisemiquavers are trilling
up there in the brain's gray atmosphere?
What melodious message from which ancestor?
(The blacksmith? The artificial flowermaker?)

Who's watching? Who's calculating your chances
if you choose a pinkish prawn in scrumptious
marzipan? Who's waiting impatiently back there
in the family tree for your marconi-gram?

Who's still got the wireless tapped into
which hemisphere, who's signalling warnings,
who's prophesying, *Come the millennium . . . ?*
What millenarian minutiae ring in your noggin,

what mildewed notions? What thorny hairtree
are relatives waving flags from? Who's decoding
solicitous semaphores flashing in the branches:
Don't go crazy, kid, it's real expensive there. . . .

Wakeful before Tests

Massachusetts General Hospital

Semesters of squandered time. Missed lectures,
stubborn childlike wandering from the subject—
is this what my body's re-living?
The self-inflicted panic of my truant years,
exhilarated horrors of eleventh hours?
Immaculate textbook pages, my clever manic notes
fractured on the unmade dormitory bed—
too late for brooding on what I should have done,
should have read, I'd make do with what I had.
Then—euphoric—I *had* nine lives!
My friends, stupefied by my survivals,
devotees of my antics, where are you now?
Could your laughter calm me?
Did it then? Girls,
this time I'm obeying instructions.
My wakeful educable body
has learned its lesson.

*

No, that's not right. Not obeying,
more, *It's too late, there's nothing I can do.*

In college, I craved extinction—
wasn't that what failure was?—
although like a magician
wrenching rabbits from a shabby stovepipe hat,
or seeming to,
I'd torch bluebooks with last-minute erudition;
I'd pass.

*

Now, behind closed lids, listening to night's
doomy sirens, I see my mother-in-law,
three months before her end:
great scared mascaraed eyes,
her perfumed negligé, the gilt rococo bed,
the champagne cashmere throw;
her friends, all *maquillage,* all mink
and dread, bending their lifted faces
to catch her clubby whisper: *Girls,*
I'm dead.

*

Of course—I'd have to think of her.
I'm haunted by her kind of terrifying
purposelessness, life looking for its mirror,
insatiable ruined desires for reassurance.

She became my education, fathomless, immaterial,
unfinished. Now, tomorrow's a hard table
I'll study on, infiltrated, pierced,
leaning into pain as into a mother's arms. . . .

*

Unfinished work, what is it?
Anonymous headlights, through-line
flashing on childhood's bedroom walls,

images I never controlled or invented,
narrating from bedroom to bedroom:
a wakeful girl afraid of the door

that opens, a young mother breathing
to her children's breath, children
another dream, another promise. . . .

*

The work.
Postponed again.
Tomorrow, a silence,
or a buzzing hive I'll enter
willingly, to belong or
else brave the smart
of its attack, to face or
lose myself in action, to do
the task I thought I came for
as I'm stung toward death.

Shangri-la

Tonight in my father's vanished house,
in the dusty upstairs hall
of my father's house that burned,

a German shepherd lies dying
in the smoky hallway, he's starving,
I know I've left him to starve though

I don't know why, so I rush to atone,
to bring him a saucer of what I have—
of cinders—though this dog who's mine,

whom I've never seen, doesn't move,
his dark heavy head won't lift
from the pine floor to the sooty bowl;

uncomplaining, unaccusing, a sorrowful
monumental dying of which I am author,
more insupportable, more wracking

than anyone I've hurt before
or abandoned; and now there's no shield
between me and anguish when I wake

to the oblivious Pacific sun;
nothing will absolve me,
my loyal dog stays with me,

the royal palm trees sway outside
the window of the Shangri-la Hotel—
day I'd have known had I not found him

Two Bedrooms

Nights I return to this room, to the faded
scarves and sachets, the rococo bed,

its pale percale sheets, the velvet chaise,
the mirrored vanity, stale exhalations

of face powder and Patou, fragrance
of the elevator, opening into 6B —

of you, operatic, negligéed, perfumed.
Here where you died, I hunt for the

thing not here, not in the faux marble
fireplace, not in the gilt frames, not

in the French night tables, nowhere
in drawers of satins and laces. Not

a hairpin or ashtray, nothing from
your collections of eyeglass cases,

lipstick cases, antidepressants. Yes,
I'm still searching for a thing to keep,

rifling your musky closets for what I'd want,
glamor you'd let go of now, let me have.

(H. M., 1988)

*

I hold to the banister,
                    picking my way
up the carpeted steps,
                    on an errand,
a rescue mission,
                    to find some "purloined"
item:
          a single jet earring, a Rose O'Neill
kewpie,
              one bronzed Shakespeare bookend —
little loose ends
              of a drama
                          that's beginning
to be forgotten. . . .
                    I know these steps,
I could climb them
                    blindfolded, barefoot,
I should know
              where they're leading:
here's my locked room,
                          the twin spool beds
I shared with a sister,
                    covered now
with Buffalo pottery
                    and cartons of china.

I walk in sleep to their
                                bedroom door
where I saw my father
                                square his gallant shoulders
one last time, take
                        one last look,
before he went down
                        for good. Here

are the bookshelves
                                of inventory, here
the ephemera,
                        postcard of presidents,
of town greens,
                        of Hitler. Here,
on the night table,
                        a crystal chimera
I handle carefully.
                        Like a safecracker
I feel each "ding"
                        with trained fingertips.
I caress while I can
                        the chipped dusty goat body,
the cracked lion head.
                        But still I don't get
what it is I came for.
                        I turn and turn
back to the stairs,
                        go down empty-handed.

(M. B., 1999)

IV

Poems

I still write them.
I imagine them lying
to anxious friends wishing me
happiness at the end of my years.
I write in the dark, always
in a state of refusal, as if
I were paying a disagreeable debt,
a debt many years old.
No, there's no more pleasure
in this exercise. People tease me:
You thought you were making Art,
you wrote for Art's sake!
That's not it, I wanted something else.
You tell me if it was something more,
or less: I think one writes
to shake off an unbearable weight,
to pass it on to whoever comes after.
But there was always too much weight;
the poems aren't strong enough
if even I can't remember a line
by the next day.

—after Vittorio Sereni

Michelangelo: To Giovanni da Pistoia When the Author Was Painting the Vault of the Sistine Chapel

— *1509*

I've already grown a goiter from this torture,
hunched up here like a cat in Lombardy
(or anywhere else where the stagnant water's poison).
My stomach's squashed under my chin, my beard's
pointing at heaven, my brain's crushed in a casket,
my breast twists like a harpy's. My brush,
above me all the time, dribbles paint
so my face makes a fine floor for droppings!

My haunches are grinding into my guts,
my poor ass strains to work as a counterweight,
every gesture I make is blind and aimless.
My skin hangs loose below me, my spine's
all knotted from folding over itself.
I'm bent taut as a Syrian bow.

Because I'm stuck like this, my thoughts
are crazy, perfidious tripe:
anyone shoots badly through a crooked blowpipe.

My painting is dead.
Defend it for me, Giovanni, protect my honor.
I am not in the right place—I am not a painter.

Air Drawing

What would be strange
in someone else's bed, familiar
here as the body's jolt
at the edge of sleep—body
persistent, solitary, precarious.

I watch his right hand float
in our bedroom's midnight,
inscribe forms by instinct on the air,
arterial, calligraphic
figures I'm too literal to follow.

I close my book quietly,
leave a woman detective to tough
her own way out of trouble—
local color of Chicago, Sears Tower,
bloodied knuckles, corpses.

I turn to him—
who else would I turn to?—
but I can only watch
for a few minutes at a time
the mysterious art of his sleep.

If I touch his hand, he won't know it,
and it's always comforted me

to feel the vibration,
the singular humming in him,
nocturnal humming . . .

My mystery falls to the floor,
nothing I'll think about tomorrow—
I'm listening for the breath
after this breath,
for each small exhalation . . .

Is this the way it has to be—
one of us always vigilant,
watching over the unconscious
other, the quick elusory
tracings on the night's space?

That night two years ago
in the hospital, tubes
in his pale right hand,
in his thigh, I asked myself,
Does he love me?

and if he does,
how could he let that steely man
in green scrubs snake his way
nearer to his heart
than I've ever gone?

Leah's Dream

". . . for she said, Surely the Lord
hath looked upon my affliction;
now therefore my husband will love me."
—Genesis 29:32

"Then finally I asked you to marry me,
my husband, and we embraced
as we never have, neither of us

breaking away from the other,
our bodies clinging,
breast to breast, sex to sex;

my arms around you, your hard hands
on my back, my face at your neck.
And you didn't break away.

When I said to you, 'I don't want
to be alone anymore,' I spoke
with the passion of an abstinent,

an ascetic hungry at last
for the world's meat and drink.
You didn't reply, you didn't pull away.

. . . Then I woke, it was still dark,
you were sleeping beside me,
snoring lightly, a small tentative sound,

like the teakettle's gentle whistle
when water begins to boil. . . ."

Then

We weren't waiting for anything to happen.
We lived by a lake, no tides to nag us,
no relentless conventions of flow

and ebb. No frantic hermit crabs
dragging sideways in their stolen shells,
nor the drained tidal pools they fled—

only the soft green surround of pine
and beech, the mackerel clouds, the meek
canoes. We felt enclosed. Safe.

The future looked fictional then,
though I never doubted a lucky life
could break, that rapture and grief

could be handed to me in one hard package,
delivered, and left, however I labored,
whether I rested, or ranted and zigzagged

from morning to evening. I worked
with my back to our life. Moonflowers
bloomed in the nightyard: white,

dazzling, sufficient to the night.

Right Now

I love the way mist fills the Common now
when warm air meets the winter's hoard of snow.
You're away. To be precise, as I need
to be more often now, you are at 8
West 8th Street. Probably. What do I know
that isn't before my eyes? March thaws; soon
we'll wake together to a diatribe
of crows. Last year's parsley will show itself,
bitter yellow-green by the curled green hose.

Is that the way *I* will learn to toughen,
wintering over whatever frost comes
to us, yet less tender than last season?
Must I survive?—I understand parsley
has no life or dread of loss to unlearn
but I do. And you—will you be here, as
right now, you are not? Though you are somewhere
as I walk doggedly into this fog,
still breathing, as you, too, are still breathing—

Keep Going

It's not only the accumulation of small slights:
your name misspelled on last evening's program;

the party uptown after the ceremonies and readings—
an editor praising C's poems as if you weren't

standing there beside him, craving appreciation
(or you *were* there, dimming, eclipsed);

then D—your loyal old friend, you'd thought—
leaving without goodbye for a midnight dinner,

clearly, you could see, forgetting you'd flown
down together, shared a Yellow Cab

from the Marine Air Terminal, checked in
to your separate funky rooms at the Gramercy;

petty distresses, trivia you're shamed to be
wounded by, the comedy of literary manners—

How to reconcile these insignificant cuts
with the weight—a boulder, really—pressing

on you as you drive (your brain still crackles
normally, well-organized signals steering

the right foot that accelerates or lifts without
thought, from the pedal), Sunday afternoon

on the Mid-Cape Highway to Provincetown:
no, the small slights aren't what's made you,

you feel, overwhelmed, despairing. There's
E's illness, her doctor calling frantically

last week, the latest test results so desperate
that specialist feared her patient was *dead;*

L's depression, months of lassitude, the trap
of his life sprung with no loophole of escape;

an "official" letter your mother just showed you,
her abandoned cottage condemned, a building

inspector demanding she take action. "Take action":
last year, when you'd nailed plywood to her windows,

hauled away the few good sticks of furniture—
even then, the neglected walls were black, mildewed,

the green daybed rich with mold, a hornet's nest
inside the door, the door lock jimmied, broken,

glistering poison ivy crawling across the floor. . . .
It's *action* she can't take, and your inaction,

watching her tough little body falter
and fail—the largeness of spirit, sacrificial

generosity you hoped for in yourself,
ceded—or unborn; and K, sweet

unathletic K, examining a box turtle
in your yard two days ago, K jaunty

in his faded red baseball cap, then—that night—
tossed in the air by a drunken car,

his face in the morgue, you're told,
unmarred, only *surprised* by the quick

skull-shattering moment of his death.
And now, you hardly notice your brain

(which you picture as hardening, sclerotic),
your brain shifting signals, so the car slows

until a passing driver yells a high-speed curse
that someone else might take as challenging,

even menacing. *Take action:* you accelerate,
again, keep going until the Sahara of dunes

on one side, the brilliant icy bay on the other,
say you're nearly here, whatever's pressing on you,

whatever rides with you, might shrink
in the scouring briny air. And like the survivor

on Everest, the photographer, oxygen deprived,
beyond cold, who stared at his teammate's body

"in perplexity," the exposed outstretched hand,
the familiar shoulder and chest, thinking,

without affect, not curiosity or grief,
How could this have happened to Rob?

his own body not having "room for emotion"
as he waited for assistance, a guide to help him

off the mountain to safety, to *life,*
his camera storing the neutral, fatal images—

like that, you can turn off the road, and pull in.

The Beach

They're not here,
the voice in the machine announced;
and then, omniscient voice:
They won't be back, ever.

But this foggy morning,
on a stony beach I'd never visited,
those patches of light—signals
from those who aren't really gone?

And then, when I reached them,
mist. As if nothing had happened.
Driftwood, white pebbles,
sandblasted bits of colored glass.

The dead:

they're not what's washed out
to sea day after day. They're absence—
lime, or ash, about to become motion
or light. But something tells me

(the tide keeps flooding me
with such wishful thoughts)

the dead will find a way—
couldn't *one?*—to signal me again. . . .

—after Vittorio Serreni

Low Tide

Tree of heaven,
the ailanthus so graceful
and disparaged. The "garbage tree."
Who notices its stubborn rhythm
in downtown alleys or gritty
abandoned lots? Junk tree,
at home in soot.

(*And why*
would I think of it
this minute, walking head down
on the flats, the peculiar hermit crabs
scrubbling away from me, manifest
hysteria in the pearly August
day?)

Undesirable now,
but once carried—precious
cargo—from China for ornament,
for shade. For its tropical attitude.
Ailanthus altissima. Last choice
anywhere other trees grow.
Limbs easily broken;

poisonous roots
invaders of drains

and wells; awful-smelling male
flowers. Allergies. Hay
fever. Disparaged,
undesirable
but still,

graceful,
if you'd look at them
with any sympathy, or hope of pleasure.
Here to stay. Here
to stay.

See how
these little crabs
haul their appropriated
snaily shells into a
blue voracious
bay

To Begin This Way Every Day

at my desk, as my friend John recommends,
   natural as, say, laughing, is for him—
      his whole household still asleep,

his elderly black cat curled
   in dawn's warm oblong of sun,
      Harry's left hand dreaming toward

his somnolent floored guitar,
   Maria's morning visions wayward as lines
      of the story she's been conjuring

for a year in her room with its vista
   of bramble, scrub oak and dunes;
      her garden flailing, the last skeletal

spidery cleomes, the splashy crimson
   dahlias lashed to their green stakes
      against the Cape's September storms.

To begin this way, to take memories
   that strum me before I wake—birth cries,
      circus elephants, Chinese rocks—that lurk

and toss in my windy aching brain,
     then fall, their familiar names set
          somehow wrong, testing me to get them

right, to make sense or song of slant
     arrangements—could I begin there now,
          weightlessly, without deliberation?

When John wasn't writing poems, he said,
     I miss the quirky way my mind works, or
          was it *the way my mind quirks?*—

This drizzly morning, I like to picture him
     at his desk in Truro, to begin to think how
          fortunate we might seem, like gamblers,

browsing and tapping the muddled alphabet
     of keys, door closed hard on the heavy day's
          commands, nerve, or nothing that nameable,

steering our hands; maybe for only one hour,
     this hour, risking what we won yesterday;
          alone, autonomous, capricious, free.

Three Provincetown Mornings

When I lift the window shade
the first blue heron, feeding alone,
stationed in the shallows.

He's early—he must be—great bird
of winter. This last week of August,
his pale face means beautiful bad news.

All summer I meant to write differently,
to find a vocabulary for the harbor,
its excitable transient birds, the dunes

where, twelve years from his death,
Thoreau wrote, *It is wisest to live
without any definite and recognized object*

day to day. Reading that late last night,
I thought, Who'd equal him for laziness?
But I knew it wasn't laziness

when I pictured him on the outer shore,
bent to his notebook, transfigured
by the cold Cape sun, each day

equal to him in interest, in variation.

*

Uninhibited, unedited, the bay
does its green job,
pale and calm as celadon.

Thousands of green species teem—
invisible pastures of plankton,
infinite food factory.

Must *everything* have a purpose?
Even the cool sand sifting
through my morning fingers?

And these hands, is there a task
they're fit for, one that matters?
My own grabbling for *gravitas*

as unapparent to the world as
oceanic life seems—
abstract, indecipherable

viewed like this from the shore.

*

Who'd argue with me if I said
the tide speaks in the voice of Horace:

*The years as they pass plunder us
of one thing then another. . . .*

I would. This tide tells me nothing—
or rather, barefoot in the sand,

I propose a voice tide never needed
as it brings in sea glass, seaworms,

"gray water" from Canadian cruise ships,
then goes back for more. People

like me, facing the bay's glistening
severity, want incident: swimmers,

silvery minnows, sailing ketches. Want
to hear an aphorism, a wave of wisdom.

Here's half a man's shoe, wet and barnacled—
I press it to my ear as if I'm listening.

Insomnia at Daybreak

So many years, so many months and seasons
re-lived in the turnings of one night:
a night of pacing, every comfortless hour
punctuated by the bells of Town Hall.
And now, why should the slow light
of morning hurt so? Like the face
of God, overwhelming, blinding—
hard, effacing face I've taken
for a mirror as the world wakes
yet again.

> *Give me the words I need,*
the words that would calm my soul,
words that would make my life work.

—*after Vittorio Sereni*

The Common (1995)

Two Worlds: A Bridge

Puffed-up windbags, black feathered bellows,
wheezy hinges: fierce yellow-eyed unlovable
inexpressibly expressive grackles.

Texas.
Oil-tainted air.
                Premonitory luxury
of leaving a life. Floating alone
at night in my air-conditioned space
capsule, unknown
for a thousand miles.

Addison Street. Dryden. Wordsworth.
Shakespeare. Auden. Swamp
mysteriously re-constituted—
a British literary map.

Banana trees. Cottonwood.
Mesquite. Blue Gum.
Tallow. Chinaberry.

Mornings at a formica table,
reading obituaries for pleasure
of the *Chronicle's* names: Pamula.
Euphie. Bubba Levine.
Billy Jo Tardy.

Was that me in the Buffalo Cafe,
laughing at death?

And walking after the day's heat,
a thousand furious grackles flaring up,
clacking, frantic at my approach,
landing—
             black iridescent blooms
in the branching candelabra
of Rice Boulevard's great live oaks.

Half a country's distance
between the body and its biography.

At first, the body's baby-ish tissue,
its nervous Boston muscles,
begged to be taken home.

But that was only the body.

I

The Acorn

On the way home from school, a child is struck
on the head by a falling acorn. She looks down
at her brown shoes, refusing to give the squirrel—
who must have waited for her, aimed at her—
satisfaction. *You've got to show them you don't care*
her mother taught her. Does this mean
the squirrel knows she's Jewish? She always
dawdles so the other girls who have friends
to walk home with won't bully or taunt her
the way the Leblanc boys did yesterday,
in front of Corpus Christi—
pulling her hair, kicking her, calling her
"kike" and "Christ killer," while Father John
strolled up and down the sidewalk
that glittered with flecks of mica, reading.
Or the way Anna and Mary, the twins, held her down
in the cloakroom to make her show them her tail,
only letting go when the art teacher saw them.
Some days, she wants to be Catholic and make
confessions. Some of the secrets she keeps
from her mother. Why hurt her and what could she do?
Don't be fooled by girls pretending they like you,
the world is full of those rotten bitches —
The acorn.

I'm a Stranger Here Myself

Sometimes when you stop for directions,
when you ask someone who doesn't look
threatening or threatened the way to a gas
station or restaurant, the person stares at you,
dumbly, or seems apologetic or guilty,
and says these words as if they'd been
scripted: *I'm a stranger here myself—,* shaking
her head, or his head, and you're especially struck
by the bond between you, your strangeness,
and the town, or city, changes to unnumbered
anonymous facades, but generic, unmistakably
New England—white clapboard houses, black shutters;
or Texas storefronts—low porches, two-by-four columns,
longhorn arches; or even Southern California,
the faces its bungalows make, the expressive mouths
of, say, Los Angeles doors—and suddenly you want
to live there, wherever *there* is, to belong
in one place, to read the surviving daily,
you want to get a grip on the local mores,
to pay taxes, to vote, you want to have cronies,
be tired together in the Stormy Harbor
Coffee Shop, to be bored with the daily specials:
you want not to be like *him,* or *her,* not the outsider
who's never sure where things are; so you say,
"Thanks, anyway," and find the worn face of a
native who'll point you to a real estate office,

which hadn't been where you were going—
But then, you stop cold, scared, wanting
only your own room, the books under the bed,
the pencils, the snapshots, what's left
of your family, the dead flies on the windowsills,
the exhausted scorched-coffee smell of your city,
familiar as your own particular dust—and you turn
on a dime, shaking off Church Street and School Street,
the allegorical buildings, the knick-knack bookshelves
in the glowing blue family rooms blind to the moonlit
Main Street night, the lonely, confused, censorious
American-ness of places you drive through, where
you can get ice cream or a flat fixed, places where
strangers get hurt, so you jump back into your car
and head out to the highway, until the town,
that stage-set that almost swallowed you,
disappears at last in the fogged rearview mirror,
and you drive to the next and the next and the next,
fleeing that vicarious life for your life.

Mensch in the Morning

He seems glad of the splay of sun and my attention;
playful but purposeful.

Chasing his tail,
he also pretends to ignore it,

then spins in the wooden cage of my chair's legs,
trapping the thing

with a fast forepaw.
Again, he snubs it, faking absorption

in some abstraction—
motes in a light shaft.

Until he lets go,
he's stuck, of course,

all his rage focussed on his caboose.
Lucky kitten,

to keep forgetting the limitations
of his choices—

is that a sign of health?
Now he sets the tail loose—

a part of him suddenly sprung free!—
then whips around to ambush himself.

In Houston

I'd dislocated my life, so I went to the zoo.
It was December but it wasn't December. Pansies
just planted were blooming in well-groomed beds.
Lovers embraced under the sky's Sunday blue.
Children rode around and around on pastel trains.
I read the labels stuck on every cage the way
people at museums do, art being less interesting
than information. Each fenced-in plot had a map,
laminated with a stain to tell where in the world
the animals had been taken from. Rhinos waited
for rain in the rhino-colored dirt, too grief-struck
to move their wrinkles, their horns too weak
to ever be hacked off by poachers for aphrodisiacs.
Five white ducks agitated the chalky waters
of a duck pond with invisible orange feet
while a little girl in pink ruffles
tossed pork rinds at their disconsolate backs.

This wasn't my life! I'd meant to look
with the wise tough eye of exile, I wanted
not to anthropomorphize, not to equate, for instance,
the lemur's displacement with my displacement.
The arched aviary flashed with extravagance,
plumage so exuberant, so implausible, it seemed
cartoonish, and the birdsongs unintelligible,

babble, all their various languages unravelling—
no bird can get its song sung right, separated from
models of its own species.

For weeks I hadn't written a sentence,
for two days I hadn't spoken to an animate thing.
I couldn't relate to a giraffe—
I couldn't look one in the face.
I'd have said, if anyone had asked,
I'd been mugged by the Gulf climate.
In a great barren space, I watched a pair
of elephants swaying together, a rhythm
too familiar to be mistaken, too exclusive.
My eyes sweated to see the bull, his masterful trunk
swinging, enter their barn of concrete blocks,
to watch his obedient wife follow. I missed
the bitter tinny Boston smell of first snow,
the huddling in a cold bus tunnel.

At the House of Nocturnal Mammals,
I stepped into a furtive world of bats,
averted my eyes at the gloomy dioramas,
passed glassed-in booths of lurking rodents—
had I known I'd find what I came for at last?
How did we get here, dear sloth, my soul, my sister?
Clinging to a tree-limb with your three-toed feet,
your eyes closed tight, you calm my idleness,
my immigrant isolation. But a tiny tamarin monkey
who shares your ersatz rainforest runs at you,
teasing, until you move one slow, dripping,
hairy arm, then the other, the other, the other,
pulling your tear-soaked body, its too-few

vertebrae, its inferior allotment of muscles
along the dead branch, going almost nowhere
slowly as is humanly possible, nudged
by the bright orange primate taunting, nipping,
itching at you all the time, like ambition.

Whatever They Want

Tonight, my students can ask me anything.
I'll tell them the story of my life,
whatever they want. Outside, traffic shimmers
in the Gulf haze, mosquitoes incubate
in the bayou. My students laugh softly
at the broad *a* of my accent, evidence—
if they need it—of my vulnerability,
a woman fallible enough to be
their mother. And it's easy, I'm easy
with their drawled interrogations,
their curiosity, the way they listen
without memory or desire every Monday,
while I peel another layer from the onion,
the tearjerker, while the air conditioner
in the classroom stirs the fine hairs
on their arms, and I forget the cool protections
of irony, giving them my suffering family,
my appendectomy, my transcendent first kisses—
What kind of teaching is this?
I transport them with me to Maine,
to the Ukraine, they see my great uncle's
dementia, my cat's diabetes—exotica
of gloom, pratfalls, romantic fantasias,
extravagant sleet, snow, sweet innuendoes. . . .
They ask for it, they want to tell me things, too,
Texas stories, with boots, with dead fathers

and shrimp boats, with malls, with grackles,
with fire ants, with ice houses, with neon,
with rifles, and the Holy Scriptures—
Inexhaustible reality!
When I drive home singing past the palm trees
and the tenebrous live oaks and the tacquerias,
I'm in the movies, and later, when I sleep,
I dream of my babies, their insatiable hungers,
I give them permission to say whatever they want,
as long as there's no meanness in it,
as long as words taste bittersweet,
as long as they're true, as long as they move me.

Desire

It was a kind of torture—waiting
to be kissed. A dark car parked away
from the street lamp, away from our house
where my tall father would wait, his face
visible at a pane high in the front door.
Was my mother always asleep? A boy
reached for me, I leaned eagerly into him,
soon the windshield was steaming.

Midnight. A neighbor's bedroom light
goes on, then off. The street is quiet. . . .

Until I married, I didn't have my own key,
that wasn't how it worked, not at our house.
You had to wake someone with the bell,
or he was there, waiting. Someone let you in.
Those pleasures on the front seat of a boy's
father's car were "guilty," yet my body knew
they were the only right thing to do,

my body hated the cage it had become.

One of those boys died in a car crash;
one is a mechanic; one's a musician.
They were young and soft and, mostly, dumb.
I loved their lips, their eyebrows, the bones

of their cheeks, cheeks that scraped mine raw,
so I'd turn away from the parent who let me
angrily in. And always, the next day,

no one at home could penetrate the fog
around me. I'd relive the precious night
as if it were a bridge to my new state
from the old world I'd been imprisoned by,
and I've been allowed to walk on it, to cross
a border—there's an invisible line
in the middle of the bridge, in the fog,
where I'm released, where I think I'm free.

Bedroom at Arles

A painting he thought would rest the brain,
or rather, the imagination—

sloped room, chrome-yellow bed,
poppy-red coverlet, his own pictures

hung askew, or painted as if they were.
He'd splash cold water from the blue basin,

then take his blue smock from the peg.
Whole days outdoors he spoke to no one,

straining, as he had to, alone,
for *the high yellow note.* . . .

Decades ago, I longed to be like him—
an isolate, a genius; beneath a poster

of his raw crooked room, I planned
a life, a monk's life, a vocation.

I was sure craziness was a side issue,
like the mistral's dust that whitened trees,

that drove him indoors to paint—
an obstacle yet, oddly, fine.

Now it seems a century's gone by
since I read his daily diary

of pictures,
that fevered year at Arles—

blue cypresses, apricot orchards,
Arlesienne faces. This bedroom.

A century, at least,
since I underestimated danger

and quarantined myself in the one room,
trying on a little madness, a little despair,

waking in the fictive mornings,
not awake yet to light like his—yellows

like sulphur, like lemons, like fresh butter,
not golden, or blazing, but homely—

Poem for Christian, My Student

He reminds me of someone I used to know,
but who? Before class,
he comes to my office to shmooze,
a thousand thousand pointless interesting
speculations. Irrepressible boy,
his assignments are rarely completed,
or actually started. This week, instead
of research in the stacks, he's performing
with a reggae band that didn't exist last week.
Kids danced to his music
and stripped, he tells me gleefully,
high spirit of the street festival.
He's the singer, of course—
why ask if he studied an instrument?
On the brink of graduating with
an engineering degree (not, it turned out,
his forte), he switched to English,
his second language. It's hard to swallow
the bravura of his academic escapes
or tell if the dark eyes laugh with his face.
Once, he brought me a tiny persimmon
he'd picked on campus; once, a poem
about an elderly friend in New Delhi
who left him volumes of Tagore
and memories of avuncular conversation.
My encouragement makes him skittish—

it doesn't suit his jubilant histrionics
of despair. And I remember myself
shrinking from enthusiasm or praise,
the prospect of effort—drudgery.
Success—a threat. A future, we figure,
of revision—yet what can the future be
but revision and repair? Now, on the brink
again, graduation's postponed, the brilliant
thesis on Walker Percy unwritten.
"I'll drive to New Orleans and soak
it up and write my paper in a weekend,"
he announces in the Honors office.
And, "I want to be a bum in daytime
and a reggae star at night!"
What could I give him from my life
or art that matters, how share
the desperate slumber of my early years,
the flashes of inspiration and passion
in a life on hold? If I didn't fool
myself or anyone, no one could touch
me, or tell me much . . . This gloomy
Houston Monday, he appears at my door,
so sunny I wouldn't dare to wake him
now, or say it matters if he wakes at all.
"Write a poem about me!" he commands,
and so I do.

May, Home after a Year Away

Bridal wreath. White rhododendron. Dogwood.
My town. At dawn, six or seven people—
hard to know if one shape's just a bundle—
sleeping on the Common's tender new grass
and on the granite benches. Dandelion
puffs cluster in the green—didn't we once
take deep breaths and blow the gossamer off
and make a wish? With each return home,
I seem to love it more, with less terror.

What would I wish for now? What wasn't working
still isn't. My friends' sorrows, mine again.
If only we could carry this sweet spring
in us anywhere . . . I hope I die in May, some
one to scatter my ashes—
                                        Is that it, Gail,
the wish you make in your happiness?

II

Bluebonnets

I lay down by the side of the road
in a meadow of bluebonnets, I broke
the unwritten law of Texas. My brother

was visiting, he'd been tired, afraid of
his tiredness as we'd driven toward Bremen,
so we stopped for the blue relatives

of lupine, we left the car on huge feet
we'd inherited from our lost father,
our Polish grandfather. Those flowers

were too beautiful to only look at;
we walked on them, stood in the middle
of them, threw ourselves down,

crushing them in their one opportunity
to thrive and bloom. We lay like angels
forgiven our misdeeds, transported

to azure fields, the only word for
the color eluded me—delft, indigo,
sapphire, some heavenly word you might

speak to a sky. I led my terrestrial brother
there to make him smile and this
is my only record of the event.

We took no pictures, we knew no camera
could fathom that blue. I brushed
the soft spikes, I fingered lightly

the delicate earthly petals, I thought,
This is what my hands do well
isn't it, touch things about to vanish.

Fracture Santa Monica

Don't walk like a drunken sailor,
my trainer scolds, as I lope across Ocean
Avenue, dreamscape of my lopsided autumn.

Odd men and women swathed in blankets applaud
when I place the broken left foot in front
of the okay right, then reverse without a hitch

and walk backwards, toward the pier,
the polluted Pacific. Why, they're applauding
my ligaments, my courage! The way I back into

traffic, the traffic signal's bird-cheeps
saving my life! They rise from their bedrolls
of stains and infirmity and the clapping

dies. *Heel, toe! heel, toe! heel, toe!*
I back through the detritus, the eucalyptus,
the *cirque du soleil* spinning behind me.

What's to be glad about or proud of
when the smallest dire injury begins
my downhill glide to self-pity, to hyperboles

of despair? I'm a parvenu, a cat-scratch
in this seascape of amputations, I'm
selfish, selfish, the trainer snaps,

What are you good for, dragging in the sand?
Who's it gonna help if you fix that foot?

The Idea of Florida during a Winter Thaw

Late February, and the air's so balmy
snowdrops and crocuses might be fooled
into early blooming. Then, the inevitable blizzard
will come, blighting our harbingers of spring,
and the numbed yards will go back undercover.
In Florida, it's strawberry season—
shortcake, waffles, berries and cream
will be penciled on the coffeeshop menus.

In Winter Haven, the ballplayers are stretching
and preening, dancing on the basepaths,
giddy as good kids playing hookey. Now,
for a few weeks, statistics won't seem
to matter, for the flushed boys are muscular
and chaste, lovely as lakes to the retired men
watching calisthenics from the grandstands.
Escapees from the cold work of living,

the old men burnish stories of Yaz and the Babe
and the Splendid Splinter. For a few dreamy dollars,
they sit with their wives all day in the sun,
on their own little seat cushions, wearing soft caps
with visors. Their brave recreational vehicles
grow hot in the parking lot, though they're

shaded by live oaks and bottlebrush trees
whose soft bristles graze the top-racks.

At four, the spectators leave in pairs, off
to restaurants for Early Bird Specials.
A salamander scuttles across the quiet
visitors' dugout. The osprey whose nest is atop
the foul pole relaxes. She's raged all afternoon
at balls hit again and again toward her offspring.
Although December's frost killed the winter crop,
there's a pulpy orange-y smell from juice factories. . . .

Down the road, at Cypress Gardens, a woman
trainer flips young alligators over on their backs,
demonstrating their talent for comedy—stroke
their bellies, they're out cold, instantaneously
snoozing. A schoolgirl on vacation gapes,
wonders if she'd ever be brave enough
to try that, to hold a terrifying beast
and turn it into something cartoon-funny.

She stretches a hand toward the toothy sleeper
then takes a step back, to be safe as she reaches.

Snake in the Grass

—I'd screamed when it slithered under my hand
as I leaned to pick the first ripe blueberry.
It was noon, a Monday in late July. The sun,
as always, was hot on my shoulders, hot
on the back of my blouse. I'd forgotten
the universe wasn't all dead pines and Indian
graves and boarded-up houses, that I wasn't
the only creature left alive in it, that I'd
never found my comfortable place inside it.
I wanted to be someone who doesn't scare,
who can't be shaken, so I wanted no witnesses
to this paradigm in the Garden. Then, the snake
slid noiselessly under the rotting porch
of our family cottage. The reduced summer woods,
the wide sky, were stunned and silent. Imagine
a silence, all you hear your own scream vanishing.
A second before, you'd knelt to the ground,
humming, and something writhed at your left hand,
wild as migraine, while your right reached
through transparent air to the first sweet berry,
treasure of asthmatic childhood's summers.
It isn't death you fear now, or years ago,
it's the sneak attack, the large hand clapped
over your mouth, bad moments that suddenly
come back when you think you're at home
in the frayed landscape you've already lost,

and a snake, a *not-you,* invisible, camouflaged
in the famished grass, jolts you out of your dream.
Try being rational and patient:
get into your car, drive down the old road
to Dunroamin' Campgrounds. You've got a quarter—
telephone a friend, he'll probably be in
his amber-lit air-conditioned office, reading
student papers. He might say postmodernism's
days are numbered, but he'd like to get away.
Tell him not to come down to the Cape.
Tell him about the harmless snake, give him
the scream, how you blushed that one of nature's
creatures should think you're a silly woman.
Embellish a little, laugh at yourself in the hot
glass booth. There'll be kids playing volleyball
on the parched field, mosquitoes, mothers
spreading mustard on baloney sandwiches.
—Wouldn't anyone have screamed at the chill
reptilian underhand move of that snake?
Wasn't that scream waiting for years?
Can't you relent, can't you love yet
your small bewildering part in this world?

Blue

Once I thought there was no blue in nature
except the sky—I thought Nature couldn't make
a blue flower, or tree, or creature.

I was young and hadn't looked at anything—

that was before I knew delphiniums
and morning glories, before I'd heard the bluejays,
or recognized the steadfast spruce trees,

or knew about Nabokov's butterflies.

Before my blue cat, I didn't know color
has its own vocabulary in every language:
his mother was a Russian Blue,

and often, when I'd been out a while,
the delirious syllables of his blueness
would amaze me at the door—

it's always so hard to remember color exactly. . . .

His coat couldn't be described by any synonyms
or tropes for gray, not mist or fog,
not colorless, not ash—

although I've buried his ashes in the pitch-
dark shade of our yard where hot summer days
he loved to lie, happy

to be cool yet close to me,

and I'm going to plant a juniper nearby,
not really to remind me, but that every autumn
the place where he lay might be

lit by the electric-blue of its leaf.

Why You Travel

You don't want the children to know how afraid
you are. You want to be sure their hold on life

is steady, sturdy. Were mothers and fathers
always this anxious, holding the ringing

receiver close to the ear: *Why don't they answer,*
where could they be? There's a conspiracy

to protect the young, so they'll be fearless,
it's why you travel—it's a way of trying

to let go, of lying. You don't sit
in a stiff chair and worry, you keep moving.

Postcards from the Alamo, the Alhambra.
Photos of you in Barcelona, Gaudi's park

swirling behind you. There you are in the Garden
of the Master of the Fishing Nets, one red

tree against a white wall, koi swarming
over each other in the thick demoralized pond.

You, fainting at the Buddhist caves.
Climbing with thousands on the Great Wall,

wearing a straw cap, a backpack, a year
before the students at Tiananmen Square.

Having the time of your life, blistered and smiling.
The acid of your fear could eat the world.

After the Storm, August

What can I learn from the hummingbird,
a big thing like me? I hardly have time
to study its flash, its momentous
iridescence, before it disappears
into the mimosa, sated with nectar.
I admire the way the greenery trembles.
I remember reading that this bird is
never sated—its whole miniature
life an exercise in digestion. What
excuse does it need to be this useless,
what's to learn from this inscrutable engine?
Why does something in me fly out
to the feathery tree, whirring
so hungrily toward translucence?

III

A Green Watering Can

It's evening.

The day visitors have come, wept,
and left their wilted flowers.
He's found a green watering can
(like mine, with a long curved spout)
tossed in a corner of the caretaker's shack.

He fills it from the empty tap—
someone has to tend these thirsty graves,
the old ones no one visits. . . .
He works haplessly, as in life,
but with sweetness and good humor,

with certainty that whatever he cares for
will thrive and grow. He smiles
his lovely weightless smile, looking
at the crooked mess of annuals
his wife left, and his daughter.

My father is telling the crickets
and the night slitherers,
Human beings never change,
but you can learn to love them.
This is the retirement he didn't live

to enjoy, where he'd impart wisdom
to his children and grandchildren
who cried pitifully when he died,
knowing now he couldn't teach them
how to become good men and women.

The dead are so efficient,
they step lightly here,
they know their way around the stones
the way the long-blind
can navigate their homes.

Here it's true nothing changes:
a hole is dug then it's filled;
a small crowd comes and always goes away.

Then my father brings out the mower
with its feathery blades. No one
likes a neat lawn better than he did,
sweating under the July sun.

I'd believe this story —
but that's not my green watering can
nourishing the hopeful dead.

Maternal

On the telephone, friends mistake us now
when we first say hello—not after.
And that oddly optimistic lilt
we share nourishes my hopes:
we do *sound* happy. . . .

Last night, in my dream's crib,
a one-day infant girl.
I wasn't totally unprepared—
there was the crib, and cotton kimonos,
not just a padded dresser drawer.

And then, I knew I could drive
to the store for the tiny, funny
clothes my daughter wears.

I was in a familiar room
and leaned over the rail, crooning
Hello, and the smiling baby—
she'd be too young for speech,
I know, or smiles—
gurgled back at me, *Hullo.*

—If I could begin again,
I'd hold her longer, closer!
Maybe that way, when night opens

into morning, and all my windows
gape at the heartbreaking street,
my dreams wouldn't pierce so,

I wouldn't hold my breath
at the parts of my life still in hiding;
my childhood's white house
where I lunged toward the flowers of love
as if I were courting death. . . .

Over the crib, a mobile was spinning,
bright birds going nowhere,
primary colors, primary
as mothering once seemed. . . .

Later, I wonder why I dreamt
that dream, yearning for what I've had,
and have

why it was my mother's room,
the blonde moderne bedroom set
hidden under years of junk—a spare room's
the nicest way to put it,

though now all
her crowded rooms are spare—

Ware's Cove

Odd, to find the little square snapshot caught
in the back of a dresser drawer:
my grandfather (I'd been thinking of him)

dwarfed in an Adirondack chair on the dock.
My father would have set him up there,
holding a bamboo fishing pole,

and had the old black Kodak ready.
It would have been a Sunday during the War.
Across the river, feverish woods

and the changing house aren't in the picture.
Nor kids, screaming and splashing
while a lifeguard dozes on his tower.

Once, when the cove was dammed,
the whole neighborhood came down
to rake the riverbed which was mined

with broken bottles. My brother's feet
and mine still bear the moon-shaped scars.
Later, a girl drowned there.

At night, I'd picture the disconnected
body, memorizing Red Cross rescues
that would never beat the river's current.

Now there's no one I love
to say what fish grandfather caught
in the not-yet polluted water,

and no one—not anyone living
in the identical, stupid houses
squeezed side to vinyl side

where the innocent woods once were—
no one can have swum here since.
There is no blue-lipped boy,

skinny and shivering, no hopeful girl,
no vigilant mother with Noxema
and towels and tears, calling her in.

Ice

In the warming house, children lace their skates,
bending, choked, over their thick jackets.

A Franklin stove keeps the place so cozy
it's hard to imagine why anyone would leave,

clumping across the frozen beach to the river.
December's always the same at Ware's Cove,

the first sheer ice, black, then white
and deep until the city sends trucks of men

with wooden barriers to put up the boys'
hockey rink. An hour of skating after school,

of trying wobbly figure-8's, an hour
of distances moved backwards without falling,

then—twilight, the warming house steamy
with girls pulling on boots, their chafed legs

aching. Outside, the hockey players keep
playing, slamming the round black puck

until it's dark, until supper. At night,
a shy girl comes to the cove with her father.

Although there isn't music, they glide
arm in arm onto the blurred surface together,

braced like dancers. She thinks she'll never
be so happy, for who else will find her graceful,

find her perfect, skate with her
in circles outside the emptied rink forever?

Traces

Sometimes I have delusions
of total recall, tyrannical, crazy.

Crazy is what I thought years ago,
"You're crazy!"
when I built a home
over my father's bulldozed house.

Nothing's ever lost to me,
certainly not the arsonned pieces of that place
that erupt like clocks
in the rockiness of my yard.

Yesterday, yellowed linoleum
bloomed in the herb garden—
his much-scrubbed kitchen tile;

and this morning, by the door,
I found a porcelain shard,
part of the upstairs bath.

Commonplace relics,
they hide themselves in a common grave,
then, break out on my path;

they bide their time, they just won't quit,
not while I live—
burnt scraps, artifacts, detritus—
they're memory's arsenal
stockpiled under sumac and ferns. . . .

A bit of blue China makes me shiver,

its graceful willow
drooping over two fishermen
pacing a broken blue bridge,

once the perfect world
I pushed and poked mashed turnips around—

Oh, unfathomable figures
so displaced below me,
so fixed in their pitiless purposes!

Phonic

As if my answering machine were a rejection,
you'd leave your forlorn message:
Call your father. . . . Then, a dial tone.
Guilty of being out, or busy,
I never thought to save the tape,
to keep some resonance and pitch of you,
if only in those four syllables—
tremulous, demanding, but tangible

as the snapshots I found today,
a torn dwarf, her plump gray face
shadowing as she squatted on our front porch,
tight braids, strange frown, white Mary Janes.

I'd forgotten that silent child
until I held her flattened image.
My peopled past is curled and tattered,
tucked into envelopes and albums;
it reconstitutes itself in dreams,
a *richesse* of repeat performances—
a friend's touch become sweetly erotic,
my children, peachy and clinging again,

you, saying you're not afraid of dying. . . .
I wish I could listen to your voice

instead of the staticky measures
of a cassette's repetitive erasures—

although sometimes in my edgy sleep,
I hear a *Gail!* that snaps me awake:
an urgent extrasensory appeal
I take for mortal emergency.
I feel sure it's you, calling
for something I don't understand
and never did. Then, it disappears.
The voice is nowhere in my wakefulness,

not kept in memory's burr—
no tender disinterested utterance
you never quite pulled off in life,
good as you were.

Pennies from Heaven

So when you hear it thunder
don't run under a tree —
there'll be pennies from heaven
for you and me!

Every time it rains,
I hear the buoyant promise of that song,
sung off-key before a shaving mirror,
or played on a scratchy RCA Victrola—
memory of someone else's memory,
the first year of his marriage, after
the Crash, after both fathers' businesses
went under. Pennies from heaven, pies
in the sky his wife always knew
not to count on. I'll hum the tune,
thinking of them in the kitchen dancing
to music from their celluloid radio,
dancing the Continental from chairs
to table to chairs like Rogers and Astaire,
style they caught on their monthly sprees
at the Bijou. Those nights they'd glide home
through the 'Thirties streets, and if it rained,
the dirty town looked lucky as new pennies.
Did they know their youth was a kind of money?
And if they knew, could they choose

how to save or use it? In a few years,
there were three babies, the War,
and the sunny, cheerful man driving
the New England territory, taking orders,
selling. They bought a house with shutters
on a river where weekend mornings
he'd croon like Crosby to his middle child,
a daughter, while he shaved, and I worshiped
from a duck-shaped potty, memorizing
the lyrics of his philosophy. Or,
tired weeknights, he'd revive if I
parroted verses he'd taught me, perfect
tin-eared imitations and together we'd warble
our hopelessly hopeful harmony. . . .
So when I hear it thunder, I don't run
under a tree—I still see our blue-green
bathroom, the closed door, the towels,
I won't let it go, that steamy scene
where I am married to my father's dreaming.

Another Tree

We sat in the yard where his house had burned.

Only I had seen the shadowed negative,
the x-ray of his brain. He squinted,

one eye too sensitive to the sun.

His right hand lay useless on his lap.
Optimism all that was left to him,

all of his grace.

For him, I'd rescued and rebuilt the place,
made a new house, planted another tree,

the little mimosa now two stories high.

In a few weeks, he'd be gone,
such was the rapaciousness of the cells,

so defenseless the nervous system.

This was the yard, this the driveway,
where one summer of Saturdays, he gathered

minyans to say *Kaddish* for his mother.

He admired every thing living, he loved
the mimosa, the pan-sized hibiscus,

the woodpecker whose staccato knocks

are the punctuation of this memory.
I held his good left hand, still the dreamer,

"Look, what a miracle this hand is — "

he said, *"seventy years I hardly used it,*
and now, the things it's learning to do!"

We looked together at what was left,
at what was growing.

Revenant

I dreamt you died again, this time in a fire.
You left a note for Mother that didn't burn,
saying how you wanted us brought up.
She wouldn't show it to me, or tell what it said.

—But I was *there* in the blazing house,
we were all there together,
although the others slept through it.

Why didn't you save yourself?
Why couldn't I save you?

You died horribly, like all those people
in runway plane crashes, seared in death,
struggling for air, piled in heaps at the exits.

Again, Mother tried to build a new life—
she bought a Japanese car, permed her hair.
Then she went into hiding.

I wandered from barber to barber
until my hair was cut short
                              as when I was twelve
and picked up the manicure scissors in the bathroom
and scalloped myself—I had to—
then hung a towel over the mirror.

Yahrzeit

Tonight, after everyone leaves, I turn
off the lights and stay in my blue chair
to watch the last embers in the fireplace,
just as I sat two years ago keeping
the flame of my father's yahrzeit candle
company when the condolence callers had gone.
Alone that night in the wing chair I spoke
aloud to the faltering flame that had become
my father and was dying. I said some words
to a framed photograph of him standing
by an airplane with his hat and briefcase,
grinning and waving like a sweet ambassador,
going I don't know where. That October of death,
my family knew only to eat and mumble and rage
to erase his body's inexorable implosions.
I'd lit the plump candle stuck in a tumbler
marked with the star of David like the plain
wooden casket my brother and I had chosen.
It flamed for days until it began to sputter
and I whispered to it as I had to him,
Let go now, you can let go, and in the frozen
living room the frail light finally gave out. . . .
But today everything—the rackety bluejay
scavenging the yard, the dun and scarlet leaves
skirmishing in the street, the pale begonias
I'd thought to rescue from the fall's first frost—

everything felt so alive, flash and color
I've been blind to these two bereft Octobers.
I wanted to grab and hold what's left to me,
to hold it all as the sun brilliantly went down,
the new moon rose. And now, while the house cools,
I lean in to urge back to life the past's
wavering warmth, to poke at the delicate ash
though I know the fire has nothing to give,
and my grief flares, and lets go, like desire.

Family Plot

I'm digging at my father's grave,
my mother's holding the rusty mums
she's carried here to make a little garden

before the first frost. Three years today,
and the grass is a damp brown rectangle
over his cryptic body that's guarded

by earth from my more morbid speculations.
Perpetual care's contracted out here,
so no one's responsible for the dried-out

tap, the graveyard's shameless posture
of neglect, certainly not this pair
of purposeful mourners with trowels

and perennials we've chosen
for their profusions of unopened buds.
I'm not good at this, thudding my shovel

at stones, setting pots in the ground
off-center. Alone, I'd plant a little dogwood,
a Japanese drift of flowering branch

above his name, but my mother sees this
as her future home and wants, as usual,
something else, something harder to nurture.

I'll never lie here. I don't want anyone
to stand, icy-handed, imagining
my ruined body. My father liked so much

to laugh—would he enjoy his clumsy girl
hacking away at clumps of sod, or his wife's
sensible blue shoes sinking in mud?

It doesn't matter. I can't even say
if he or I believed in God,
or in any kind of hereafter. . . .

A drizzle mists the raw new hole,
mists the one white rose from my table,
and the pebble I place on his headstone

like a good Orthodox daughter
leaving a memorial relic
as if it were a talisman of devotion that

nothing—no eternities of neglect by
myself or others, no drought or blight
or storm or holocaust—could erode.

IV

Foliage

Even the man who dozes on cardboard
in the Common, wearing a bright knit cap,
has picked Clover and Ladies' Thumb to stick
in the cosmos of his shopping cart.
These last warm days, wanting to deny
what's frozen and gray ahead, I admire
the star turns of my town's great trees.
Sunbursts, and the alizarin crimson

of our maples' explosions, a kind of payoff
(I want to think) for all the dying,
yet something I'm part of—part of me—
like my feet, planted deferentially
in this old park, my hands red at my sides,
my head nodding and shaking in the leafy air.

The Common

Iron cannons from the Revolution. Ghost music—
folk songs, rock concerts, Sunday demonstrations.
A granite slab for the elm where Washington

took command. A new wood plaque, already rotting,
for Margaret Fuller Ossoli—the city fathers'
minimal nod to the life of her mind.

The black trunks of old maples brushed with snow,
their strong lines rephrased by snow's finery.
From a concrete gazebo, Abraham Lincoln

gazes down at the cobbled plaza where raffish
bands plugged in, and stoned crowds gathered;
my small son and daughter skipped ahead

of me, hand in hand, to the swings, the jungle
gym, the roundabout, and at home, pre-season
jonquils dazzled in a white crockery jug.

Stringed beads—necklaces, earrings—for sale
by a woman who's sat cross-legged on folded blankets
since those days, those days.

The season's worst cold brewing this early morning.
Two men huddled in damp sleeping bags spread out
on newspapers; convulsive dreams of their war.

The oaks. The maples. In the near-zero day
I take on faith, faith in Nature, that life's
machinery groans and strains in the frozen limbs.

At Boston Garden, the First Night of War, 1991

Dank rank North Station.
Sausage and peppers, pizza, beer
in big waxed paper cups. Wet floors, wet wool coats.

Oily franks gleaming like trophies
on an overlit rotating grill. The last
rush-hour trains shaking the floor. Five minutes

since the first news, from TV's
hanging, hospital-style, from the ceiling.
Inside the Garden, on the fringe,

we sidle close to the athletes, measure
ourselves against the startling height, the players
warming up, hookshots, dunks, none

of the boyish joking and jostling.
Amplified organ music: *Yankee Doodle Dandy.*
Over There. This is the Army. Out here

in America, a crowd gathers for gratification,
for pleasures, then stirs and is stirred by songs.
Loudspeaker introductions and

"A moment to honor our fighting men and women."
Star Spangled Banner, trumpet flourishes:
And the rockets' red glare, the bombs bursting in air —

applause, tentative at first, then explosive.
(The body's sly, shy intelligence so easily confused.)
The words, lightbulbs blinking on a scoreboard.

Poem Ending with Three Lines of Wordsworth's

The organ donor who smiles
in the leathery dark of my wallet
from a driver's license

has already struck one woman—
elderly, confused—
who stumbled off a Somerville curb

one January dusk
and became a sickening thump,
then a bleeding body

cradled in the driver's arms
until police and ambulance came.
That old woman lived

to sue the driver who now
takes a different route each week
to the supermarket,

and on her birthday,
in line at the Registry, decides
she's old enough, if not

for a Living Will, then to leave
her kidneys or heart or liver;
the little silver label below her

Polaroid portrait is the Registry's
donor code. She envisions herself
extricated one night

from crushed burning metal
by the jaws of life
less lucky, finally, than her victim

whose two pocketbooks (maybe
she was a pursesnatcher?) flew
in opposite directions

and landed awfully far
from the eyeglasses and left shoe.
All the eyewitnesses

exonerated the driver.
They swore to what she won't remember:
the old woman fell,

or fainted to the fender;
the car was going five miles an hour.
Still, that impact was what she'd dreaded

all her tremulous years at the wheel
which she grips for dear guilty life,
concocting terms of a bargain—

she'll bequeath what she's got in her body
so whatever virtues she lacks,
she won't just be someone dead

unprofitably traveling toward the grave
like a false steward who has much received
and renders nothing back.

Lilacs on Brattle Street

On the brick sidewalk, pale clusters
of purple stars, picked carelessly
from nineteenth-century yards
by rootless flirtatious students,
tossed away, darkening, after a brief fling
with nature and the city's literary past. . . .

Brattle Street. "Tory Row." This afternoon,
I could almost think nothing's changed—
clouds of May cherry blossoms, pink dogwood,
the mellow blown tulips—so peaceful,
Longfellow himself might be strolling here,
lost in Dante, *nel mezzo del cammin . . .*
or Margaret Fuller, her father's only son,
breaking from studies in Greek and Latin,
not yet awakened to love, not yet drowned. . . .

A small boy tears past me, his arms full
of lavender plunder, lilacs he's bringing home
for his mother. I like his face
on which little but joy is written,
yet I have to invent a darkness in it,
as if, moments ago, he was dragging
his sneakered feet, desperate to forget
what his teacher said, something about Chernobyl.
She pointed to it on the roll-down Hammond map.

He was swept for the first time by the question
What if nothing lasts?

I make this innocent boy, this thief,
think my thoughts about nuclear ash
blowing across Kiev, across our ancestors.
I see him in the stunned classroom, terror
that passes when the bell rings, but we know
it will return now, over and over,
the too-bright light, eye-widening
what if—

what if everything in his world that matters
were colorless, empty, gone
like the wooden synagogues of Poland,
everything—the Victorian schoolhouse,
its airy unfair cage of gerbils; the 5&10
where he buys his models; his sister,
his sister waiting for him now on the front steps;
the houseplant his mother named for him yesterday
while she watered it—*Begonia*—its pink flowers
in the front window beside the gray cat
watching for him, too, planted there,
we think, since morning, since he left for school—
reliable, wily;
                    and his room upstairs,
his Marvel comics, his painted bookcase,
the plastic dinosaurs lined up on its shelves
like disguised lead soldiers—the fierce
triceratops, the mastodon, the inchling
woolly mammoth—replicas he loves from the set
his grandfather *May his soul rest in peace*
sent him last year . . .

A Small Plane from Boston to Montpelier

This twelve-seater wanders west of my childhood,
my used-up river snaking away
beyond the tinfoil wing;

ahead, the raking late afternoon,
the spiritual mass
of New Hampshire's mountains.

Isn't this how Bierstadt saw, and the others,
from horseback, or on foot,
when they set their easels up a century ago—

the light,
like a signal they believed in,
illuminating the stirring, snow-brushed peaks,

man in the landscape
tiny as a thistle.

What they'd fled—
the machine of the nineteenth century—
bucolic to us now,

and their God—
didn't he illuminate then
the implications of the cycles,

or,
promise something paradisical? . . .

This silvery pod,
hurtling past the clouds,
barely keeps us from the cold,

its wall a membrane icy to the touch,

and below,
a tiny plane like this one
zooms diagonally to its destination.

from **The Pose of Happiness (1986)**

Mashpee, 1979

The elements of the day aren't in accord:
warm sun on my hair, a blue spring sky,
the scorched holly and pines.

Where the low gray house stood,
nothing but metals and charred wood.

Better if it had vanished completely,
the fairy tale where I make one greedy wish
too many: *to have things just as they were* —

and then wake, stupefied,
to an empty space.

I can't say goodbye to this litter
of bricks, the twisted frigidaire,
our blackened bathtub
that sprawls in the foundation . . .

My parents stand by the rhododendron's
ghastly lace, showing the insurance detective
their few snapshots—

On the wide screenporch
overlooking the lake,
we hung Japanese lanterns one anniversary—

the picture shows five cousins, the picnic
table, candles flaming on the gaudy cake.

Mashpee, 1952

Dawn at the lake's edge.

In the glowing mist,
a lone fisherman—
my father—rowing in
with his catch of perch,
or pickerel, or nothing—

Or evenings, walking
in a headcloud of gnats,
the quiet road, blackberries
and wild roses, stars
waiting behind the mauve sky.

That summer, I grew into
a wide dimness, dreamt
of the family atom split,
a grandparent or sister
leaving, never returning—

In August, we were cooled
by the lake's breath,
listened witlessly
to a blurred radio report
of Boston's heatwave.

And friends—long dead now—
mother's friends sprawled
gratefully on the porch,
reading easy Ellery Queens,
shades down in the rooms upstairs;

and the children,
lying on the porch floor,
pooling their decks
of playing cards, played
endless games of War . . .

After the Fire

I wake sometimes thinking, it's still there:
my father's red lumberjacket still hangs
on a hook in the back hall;

in the dining room, the veneer still
blisters and cracks on Aunt Belle's
upright piano. Dampness has made it
hopeless, forever out of tune;

a blue platter hangs above the mantel:
If music be the food of love, play on!
it orders us in blue calligraphy
around its unglazed border.

We were so unmusical.

Dumped in the country,
the old piano was usually ignored.
Once, my cousin, visiting
from his cheerful, sensible life,
groaned at the sound,

but that night he played us
his romantic repertoire—
*Stranger in Paradise, I'm a Fool
to Want You, Tenderly*—and we sang

off-key together
as Aunt Belle's piano,
getting the words
absolutely foolishly right . . .

That gleeful group of singers
must have been what my young parents
hoped for, buying a summer cottage
on the Cape right after the War . . .

As my cousin prodded the swollen keys,
the breeze moved up from the lake,
stirring the embers in the fireplace,
this deceptive flutter of my memory,

my family standing, joined
around the ruined instrument—

It wasn't music, really,
but we played on.

Ruins

The year my father bought the place,
a forest fire burned so close
it ate the outhouse, scorched the oaks.
We came, to explore the foundations
of cottages and old estates,
sit in the charred skeletons
of a tycoon's antique Fords.

Like scholars, we sifted the absent
neighbors' residue for souvenirs—
when I found Dutch iceskates,
I felt foreign, and fictional.

The damaged wilderness was ours
those brilliant dreamy week-ends.
My mother picked black-eyed Susans
and Queen Anne's lace for the table.

She dug a sassafrass tree
and replanted it in our yard.
We planned to make medicinal tea,
like the Wampanoags had brewed here,
from its green mitteny leaves.

That house held us so, we broke apart,
departed, one child following another

in a fury of independence—the family,
like milkweed in autumn, finally burst
from its pod and disappeared, scattered
to other locations, dislocations . . .

Now I cross the seared lawn
to join my parents; the arsonist
hovers here with an awful presence.
Mother, Father, what's ours in this
rubble? When they come to pick *us* over,
what will they find here, what did we leave?

Mashpee Wine

The barn still stands, but barely,
the roof's half gone, the walls
curve inward, windows slanting
without their panes. The wooden
floor has rotted; I can see
the hump of sandy dirt beneath it—
nothing left to save.

I tell the builder to tear it down.

The water tower, the pump house—
the house itself—have already
disappeared, their histories
undocumented, half-understood.

Years ago, when we brought
the tower down, we found it
littered with squirrel skeletons.
I used to bring my grandfather
tall, cold glasses of that water
as he sat in the sun, waiting.
"Mashpee wine," he called it.

Was it the drowned animals
that made it so delicious?

I'm nervous in the barn, afraid
today's the day it will cave in.
It's all shadows and a bit of light,
wind tears through the holes.
It smells of mildew, and worse.

Someone has dragged a damp
kingsize mattress to a concave
wall; beside the "bed," a 3-legged
chair (discarded from the vanished
kitchen), a sloping table;
the floor's been swept. A straw broom,
worn to a nub, leans at the former door.

The bed's so neatly arranged,
with matching sheets so neatly
tucked, I imagine hospital corners.
"The back seat of a car was good
enough for me," the builder laughs,
shaking his head—

but I think of these kids
so desperately domestic, snuggled
here in their fragile lair—love
isn't love without a place
to pretend to live. "The world
is a bridge," the Persians said,
"build no house upon it."

Tomorrow, this wreck comes down.

My father's given me the land.
To construct a house—to make

accommodations. . . . We walk out
to the scar that looks too small.
The porch goes here, I tell the man,
the kitchen over there. Up on the hill,
he drives the markers in.

Reading Akhmatova

This morning I went into the woods
to find a beech tree of my childhood.
Gray-limbed, motherly and capacious,
it once seemed to me the only place
to brood over my mournful lucky life.
It was still there, but leafless,
not much taller than myself. I leaned
my cheek on a cool dead branch
and stood that way a while until
my own mawkishness embarrassed me—
the way I always lament these small
inexorable shifts in the ecology.
So I walked down the hill, my feet
crunching in the dry beech leaves,
and swam in the old lake, holy
as the world's past. Only a family
of mallards was swimming there, moving
toward shore until they sensed me
and turned and glided away,
their feet making a frantic stir
under the water's surface.

I've lost no one.
Not my mother, alone today
under anaesthesia, my frail father
waiting here by the phone, my son
and daughter thousands of miles apart,
thousands from me. Last night I woke
again and again, heard my gray cat
scratching to get out, and kept him in.
I'm ordinary—my fears are ordinary.

Next Door

Snow trims the dead elm and the black
fire escape. Against the chill sky,
the red roof burns through a skim
of white. Bills and sympathy notes
accumulate behind the flat door.

The history of the house is hidden
to the eye—the alarm in the attic,
the glitter of a decade's argument.
Standing at my bedroom window,
I want to know nothing—

less than I know:
a woman loved a man, and other men.
The strange traffic of a world
coming apart. The blackness
that filled the rooms one night,
the sharp ring at the end.

We sat in the yard one summer
afternoon, calling over the fence
to a neighbor already dead.
A tiger cat miaowed at the door;
I caught and held her, wondering.

Now the cat's mine.

You're beside me here at the window,
shivering sympathetically. Together
we go over the details. We do it
until I recover. Each telling begins
my education again. I want to know
nothing less than I know.

Fallen Angels

I almost died last night eating shrimp.
That's how they diagnosed it
at Mount Auburn Emergency after
they'd shot me full of adrenalin.
My heart fluttered, I couldn't keep
my hands still, and I laughed and cried
like a crazy person, my face swollen
with hives, my throat closing.

"I don't look like this,"
I insisted to an intern who
wasn't interested in my looks,
just whether I kept breathing.

Now everyone in the family's impaired.
Even my brother hears whistling
when he walks down his own hallway—
nowhere else. There aren't any windows,
so it's not the wind, and not tinnitus—
his ears only whistle in the one hallway.

We're used to his peculiar ailments;
he's our genius. Last year,
he was sure his face was falling.
And before that, for months he couldn't
read, or see in his microscope.

He thought his nose was beginning
to block his vision. An ophthalmologist
at the Health Plan said his eyes were
"normal."

We're what I used to call
"discombombulated."

To forget our troubles,
I go every night to a different *film noir.*
Sometimes my brother comes along.
We want to see a hapless loser
we can't identify with,
and some stylized violence—
Dana Andrews, grabbing women
too hard, and talking without moving
his thin, cruel lips; John Garfield
(before the blacklist), corrupted
because he grows up on the Lower East Side
and becomes a boxer and loves money.

We laugh dispassionately at Linda Darnell,
plump, coarse, contemptuous of men
as she pours coffee in a crummy diner—
Pop's Diner—every unattractive man
in town (population 4,000), including
Pop, slavering over the counter at her,
putting nickels in the jukebox
to play "Fallen Angel" again and again,
so the music's still going,
somewhere,
later when they find her dead.

Night after night,
I walk through the icy streets
of Cambridge, my home town,
the city I was born in. The neon
sign at the Holiday Inn is always
half-lit. In the bars, people
smoke cigarettes as if their lives
were a Fifties movie, and cancer
and coronaries couldn't afflict them.
Lucky for me
this town shows so many old movies.
I keep busy, work all day,
eat grains and vegetables, feed my cats,
swipe a sponge across the counters—
then, the entertainment. I know
there's something out there shady enough
to keep keeping me distracted.

In the Dark Our Story

                        is still unwinding.
It's 1919, the train's dropped us
in the Panhandle. This landscape
is only for the Farmer's pleasure.
We're stick figures, black things
moving in a sunlit picture.
How we love is our only secret.

The Farmer watches me hour on hour
from his velvet chair beside the field.
You say it's clear what he's thinking.
You say, *Marry him,* he'll die soon,
anyway.

            What can I do—futility
burns in me in the blazing noons;
it's no blessing to be pretty
if it's impossible to be good.

I marry him.

He gives me everything—
a gilt piano, silk dresses,
pears served on a silver plate.
He gives me tenderness, and sometimes

the streaking sunsets make me
strangely happy.

Stuck with our plot,
I tell him you're my brother;
you move into the house to wait.
We three take meals together
on the sunporch; my husband
seems to be growing stronger.

Eyeing the rich wheat fields
we're dangerously lazy,
and together at table, nervy.
It can't last,
me loving you both, and defenseless.

Tonight he flies at you in rage—
over nothing really—your kissing me
in the gazebo; mightn't a brother do *that?*

I think when sound is re-invented,
someone will make a movie of this:
a soft-focus evening, the goldgrained air
turned ashes and black metal, hard knives
flashing, cutting our lives to pieces.

He couldn't touch me without touching me.

In the dark of my story,
you'll both be dead. This has to happen—
I can't signal the cameraman to stop.

All I know of passion is in the film
where I stand between you two,
afraid to move, and happy—

no, not *happy,* but in the pose of happiness
I've seen in pictures . . .

In the Garment District

Nothing like 10 in the morning
for making love—cats glaring
from the table opposite, the dog
watching gloomily from the rug,

and after, opening cans
of their food, you in the shower
singing while elevators ring up
through the sidewalk, carrying
their racks of dresses, the noises
of ordinary business:
unloading, loading

Later, I stand at the window
watching a man in an office
through the arc of gold letters
that spells HESS REAL ESTATE.
He goes through his daily routine,
removes his brown jacket,
places it in a gray file drawer,
rolls up his sleeves.

And then, in the distinct light,
he stares down at the traffic.

He might, in his white shirt,

be wondering how to fill the day
but he's perfectly still. He might,
framed in the arched window, be part
of a Hopper painting, precise,
painful, not quite come to life—
the empty office, file drawers,
a bald man with nothing to do,
staring inward in the hard light . . .

And I know this memory of 20th Street
will come back often in the years
after we leave the city: bright sun
flooding the morning loft, you and I
loving, our animals arranged around us,
industry clanging on the sidewalk,
and across the street, a middle-aged man,
motionless, not quite anonymous.

A Deck of Cards

This chorus girl was pensive,
Sadness was on her brow,
Till she met her Sugar Daddy,
And she's ex-pensive now!
                    —from a Vargas queen of hearts

When Mister Mulryan called me into his office
to "show me something," I was lucky—
all he flashed was playing cards,
nude women in white cowboy hats,
one with a curving fishing rod and net.
I was eleven, no one could blame me
for confusing sleazy glamor and sex
and keeping it to myself, for finding
a goatish camera salesman romantic.

My father would have fired him
and avoided me for days.

At home, I took to the darkened den
and watched TV, old as I was
for Howdy Doody, and contemptuous
of Big Brother Bob who cursed one day
when he thought the microphone was off.
My father suffered, never to find me

waiting in the hall. The love I wanted
came late at night, after he'd left me
to lie in my spool bed, as my sister
in her spool bed slept the sleep
of someone still a child. Then I met
my 2-dimensional man, nasty in his cowboy hat
and spurs, dangerous with a dangling cigarette.

Only my grandfather saw me change,
watching from the hardship of retirement.
"Hedy Lamarr!" he called me, or "Veronica Lake!"
when my hair fell softly in my face.
Then I looked in the mirror and thought:
"*Pretty?*" I pretended headaches and sore throats,
stayed home from school, wandering voluptuously
from my bed to the overlit bathroom
where I preened with rouge and Shalimar perfume . . .

The next year I was taller
than half the boys in school.
Too awkward suddenly for baseball
with my brother's friends, I borrowed
a canoe and paddled on the Charles
to meet a destiny Thoreau had never
recognized. Sunk from the transcendental
mores of my favorite stories, I floated
on the dirty river, where toughs in rowboats
flirted across the waterlilies. Flattered,
ignorant, I paddled the term away.

In seventh grade, we traded dog-eared
books we didn't read but hid, and peeked at.
My Beginning Latin teacher confiscated one

from me, and blushed. I kept a diary
that Mother couldn't see . . .

Gallia est omnis divisa in tres partes.
I was divided, too—what use was Caesar?
I waited for my body's lines to curve,
remembering verses from Mulryan's deck
as I skipped home from school, mouthing
racy words, happy knowing everything is secret—
luscious secrets I'd never learn to keep.

Teeth

Where are my teeth?
my grandmother asks the room.
It's early Sunday afternoon;
her eyes explore the walls for reply.

She's asked four times today
in her new, thin voice.
Doc's been gone a year. That morning,
she heard pigeons at the window—
The doves were wooing all night,
she complained at the funeral home.
I wasn't sure she knew who died.

"Here they are," I answered every Sunday,
handing her the big black pocketbook.
She searches for dentures
and her change purse, pinned inside.

Reddish-blonde still, still almost
beautiful, she speaks fearfully
of coming here—*here* is our house,
or America—

At 17, she taught in a one-room
school in Maine, cramming each night
the math she'd never studied.

In a photograph, a dramatic portrait
from an amateur theatrical in Lincoln,
she was stylish, like a Gibson Girl.
American.

But she couldn't go on the stage:
it wasn't *nice.*

Where's my bag? she pleads
though it's in her lap.
Yesterday, she flushed a dollar bill
down the toilet. She meant to hide it.
She's forgotten that.

The stories she told are still intact:
the shaky escape from Vilna;
her courtships, inappropriate except for Doc
who had a dental practice;
her mother's stroke: great-grandmother
tried to smother the children—
my mother, my uncle—
to hide them from Boston's Cossacks.

But now she can't tell them anymore,
spilling her change in the living room.
She doesn't see the woman I become,
or see my girl—
who's going on the stage—
as she scrubs our copper roasting pan
brought over on the boat;

or my son,
who enters now, fresh from Jack's Joke Shop,

and opens a little red cardboard box
to show me a set of Chattering Teeth.
He turns a tiny key to wind them,
and off they go,
clacking mindlessly across the old oak table.

Being Sick

for Catherine Murphy

The pleasure in it diminishes.

Once, propped on fresh pillows
in my sunny bedroom, the yellow
flowered wallpaper, cats at my ankles
under the blankets, Ma Perkins
on the bedside radio, sounds
no one else I knew was hearing—
paradise was a mild virus.

Over six years of grammar school,
a whole year missed, at home.
Those one hundred-eighty days
should have earned me a malingering
prize at graduation. I'd wake
to the nostalgic soreness
in my throat, or head,
and could sink back into bed—

and the asthmatic nights in the country
when my father lit the fire,
put a kettle to steam on the logs,

and held me—*breathing*—on his lap
inside an army blanket tent.

To be sick, to be so loved . . .

Now the rewards diminish.
My face in the bathroom mirror,
ugly yellow smudges under my eyes,
reddened nose, memories of invalids
who didn't recover.

The cat prowls around my bed, unfed,
restless. A city plow burrows
up the frozen street, disabling
the cars. I should be up, working,
not watching an icicle
that cracks now at my window
and sinks into the snow.

Elementary Education

After recess, we file into the hall
in a Victory Stamp line, ready
to fight Hitler and Hirohito
with Standing Liberty quarters
and Mercury dimes. We stick
serrated squares into our books—
pictures of the Minute Man,
licked almost clean.

Then the art teacher arrives,
with her box of slimy plastolene.
Sitting crosslegged on the floor,
I roll fat pieces of clay
into snakes between my palms,
coiling eels to make a perfect bowl.

In the amber afternoon
of Miss McGreevy's classroom,
I think biography's the same as history,
and I plan my bowl's unearthing
years from now—*thirty,* maybe—
from my casket. I see my grown-up
dress, nail polish on my perfect oval nails.

I'll die of measles—
or a broken heart. A man who looks

like General MacArthur or the Father
of Our Country pushes past the family
at my grave and takes me away . . .

The art teacher's fragrance is different
from Miss McGreevy's or my mother's.
She lost her husband in the War.
Her fingernails are long, and painted black.

At the end of class, my bowl
will be an ashtray, or a loopy ball.
I forget—do I want to be an artist?
I can't think what I'd put inside the frame.
—I *won't* grow up to be a mother.

When I'm thirty, I'll be a famous painter—
silly to think anything else.

At two o'clock we write short stories.
I'm proud of my round obedient penmanship.
I announce, I'm going to be an author,
then dip my pen in the inkwell.

I'm a writer until the bell rings.

The Horizontal Man

Surely it was too awful to be real. The
darkened library, the buildings full of
empty classrooms, the threatening olive-
green shape of the mailbox under the lamp
at the centre of the campus . . .
                    —Helen Eustis, *The Horizontal Man,* 1946

On the second page,
my old professor's murdered with a poker.
His black curls, matting with blood
on the shabby rug,
                    were wild and gray
when he lectured to the Shakespeare class
on Sputnik and Ophelia. We'd all heard
of his affairs, and of this novel,
already out-of-print, written by a former wife

who killed him with a pen—revenge
more cruel than alimony
to young things on allowances . . .

When he recited "O, what a rogue
and peasant slave am I," we thrilled
to the alcoholic timbre of his brogue . . .

This reissued mystery
brings the whole semester back.
Fat, and pining for a boy,
I ate and smoked and slept most days away,
convinced I'd end up lonely, and alone.

For Professor F, I studied
"O that this too too solid flesh would melt,"
and earned the isolated A that failed
to keep my parents' hopes for me alive.

I recognize the Infirmary—
it's at the end of Paradise Road.
The demented freshman's dragged there
in the second chapter, babbling about love;
the nurse thinks she's the "perpetrator."

I remember the unwomanly physician
stricken by the vagaries of menstruation—
Is the psychiatrist from Springfield
the one they called the night my mind
was slipping, and the dean suspected
that wasn't all I'd lost that term?

In the spring nocturnes of my sophomore year,
I lay on my restricted cot,
confined to campus for my indiscretion—
my confession. I memorized soliloquies
for Doctor F—"To be or not"—
as if my life depended on my memory.
There was nothing I was going to *be* . . .

My teacher died, exhausted,
in a rest home late last year.

I've read all night again.
This *roman à clef,* with its bloody weapon
on the cover, is like the dream I stay up
to avoid, the classic college nightmare:
a gothic building, and months
of literature unread, the unversed girl

I never stop becoming, dragging
her cold feet through the scrollery
iron gate, past Paradise Pond
to the examination hall silently
filling with victims and perpetrators.

Jewelweed

We were talking about sex, taking
the dirt road to town, walking
slowly in the hot afternoon.

I hardly saw the fields
shimmering in the heat, the goldenrod's
itchy impressionist glow,

the pale touch-me-not,
or jewelweed, blooming in shade,
so skewed was my vision,

so interior. That day we agreed
never to touch each other,
passing the warm brown beds of pine

needles, the tiny graveyard. My face,
your face, reddened in August's ardent
flush; our hands clung to their pockets.

That conversation seemed harmless—
strange, that I still need
to put it this way—

Anyway, it must have been too far
to town. We turned back at a stone
marker to join our friends swimming

in a black pond deep in our past.
Now I am in the future where nothing
has happened, nothing happens.

What were we walking toward
that prickly summer day,
both of us suddenly guarded,

uneasy strangers, or greenhorns,
or children transported unprepared
to a heartless institution?

Pears

gone suddenly from the pear
tree, wrapped in tissue by the woman
next door, whose daughter never visits,
who'll give the fruit to her neighbors
finally, and some will be grateful
and some will shake their heads,
and a small boy will spit a piece
of pear on the sidewalk, hating
the skin, as the woman shuts the gate—

and I'll watch all this
from the window of my furnished room
this fall, conscious of my body,
and of my mother's pear tree,
the bushel baskets in the cool cellar
packed with tissue-wrapped pears,
and her own mother, blind,
frightened, not senile enough—

my grandmother, alone
in a tiny room in the nursing home,
waiting for her daughter's visits
which were daily and dutiful,
slipping in and out of sleep,
her scattered children, beautiful dead
sisters, her father the peddler,

and crazy mother, a huge dark boat
crossing the ocean, *the Old Country,*
copper pans, Sabbath candles
lit in brass candlesticks—

my grandmother, waking just once
at the end in her watery green room,
hearing her weeping daughter, saying
That's all right, I don't mind —
her words hum for a moment
in my cells, like the bees
homing in on the sweet rotting
fruit fallen by the pear tree
as the old woman, graceful in her
wasted giving, turns from the gate.

Early Winter

I wake in the rubble, not of war,
but an untended room. December.
The furnace is off.

Mornings, I taught my children
you rise and buckle your galoshes,
and face the world's great offerings.

I taught them as fast as I could,
barely holding my intelligence
a minute before passing it on.

After school, my boy played
in the warm kitchen afternoons,
cinnamon spicing the gloom.

I miss the simple expectation
of those days—departures
all followed by returns.

On the bedroom floor, a heartshaped
stone I took from the Sandwich beach
last summer. Gray and pink, cold,

it's the size and shape of my daughter's palm.

When you lose touch, I declare
to the grubby room, and then drift off,
not finishing my sentence.

Cold air, I'll learn to love you yet,
shake memory back to its place
so I can straighten up.

Memory, the last thing I'll put away.

Anomie

Gray morning and the first snow
spends itself at the sidewalk.
A man on a slate roof
clears leaves from gutters,
his visible breath
the calligraphy for *cold*.

Gray everything but his red jacket.

Quiet pervades the houses,
men and women at their offices,
children at school or still unborn.
The cats, left alone,
seek the mean warmth of radiators.

You, too, disappear into the day,
easy as opening a door—

Where would I want to go?
I board a bus where passengers
lose themselves in the tabloids,
their hands graying with newsprint.
Crimes of passion in Montana
stir my crazy yearning to confess.

I want to go nowhere: no counterfeit
paradise, palm tree at the patio edge.
No old European city demanding
I enter its museums and theaters.
No sultry nights on the savannah.

Black trees pass in a blur,
the Germanic Museum, the coin laundry,
the Home for Little Wanderers.
Snow thickens at the window
as we pull into the terminal,
the opening wedge into emptiness.

Norumbega Park

A pink motel hovers over the river,
Shangri-la where local athletes
purchase local women in the lounge . . .
Is this where I grew up?

I paddle in my Oldtown canoe,
looking for relics of riverbank
that pre-date highway and turnpike.
Blackberries ripen by the black water,
a snapping turtle suns on a rock,
suspicious as his relatives, years ago.

In the Fifties, an amusement park
lured and lowered the neighborhood.
Summer nights, sucking in our breath,
we scraped under the chain-link fence
to Abbott & Costello and Boris Karloff
flickering in the mosquitoed dark.

The tumbling seats of the lindyloop
up-ended us until we were loose
with fright and shrieked to be let off.
None of us risked the rollercoaster,
or the two-headed boy,
or the man who ate live hens.

Freaks were like dead men—
we might be changed by seeing them.

We crouched and fed the ducks instead.
Or, invaded the Penny Arcade
for licorice and cotton candy
and postcards of the Hollywood stars.

Sticky and spent, I gathered Paramount
faces from the scuffed floor,
and brought John Hodiak and Lizabeth Scott
home to join Jeff Chandler
in a shoe box on the shelf.

I didn't know enough to save them;
they'd be collectors' items now.

Nobody saved the ballroom, its wine
velvet loveseats and gold brocade,
the carousel horses or the ferris wheel.
Or the moody brown bears
wandering in a limitless green field.

I watched them through barbed wire,
unnatural dangerous creatures
so resembling men they seemed
like coarse imposters, criminal.

But they were only unlucky animals,
out of place, like the brown mallard
who floats by me on the murky river,
her five ducklings swimming
secure in their artless childhoods.

Daylight

Sometimes the body loses faith
in the body. It's got nothing
to cling to then. Like the feeling
when you unlock the door
to your rooms, unsuspecting,
and notice the drawers not closed
quite right, and pulling them out—
yanking, really—you find all
the little jewelry boxes opened.

Grandpa's gold pocket watch,
a Chinese locket, jade earrings
you loved—all *gone,*
not having left the slightest
impression on their tiny cotton beds.

After a robbery, the physical
falls away. The detective tells you
there's nothing to wait for,
nothing will be recovered.
What's left must be spirit,
or the life of the mind—

or the will to turn outward,

to focus on the corporeal world
outside: a gray cat
in the neighbor's driveway stupidly
sniffing at a trembling squirrel,
the squirrel's bravura attempt
at escape—*Safe!*—
Kitty's tame confusion.

A small boy rides his tricycle
in circles on the broken sidewalk.
Blue morning glories scale
their taut white strings.
Someone drives off in a borrowed van,
the side windows painted, or decal-ed,
preposterous mauve and lemon sunsets;
one tail light's smashed.

Across the street, two dogs,
one black and white, one golden,
romp in the radiant abandoned lot.

Hurricane Watch

The power was off.
We cleared dishes from the table.
Shutters crashed against the windows.
Below us, in the lake, the minnows
were in a frenzy. Limbs cracked—
one great tree smashed to the ground.
Leaves flew past, pasted themselves
to the panes. Somewhere,
my father was on a train.

The blue walls quaked,
too weak to hold the roof up.
Telephone lines were dead.
We had no batteries for the radio.
Our neighbors weren't our friends—
we couldn't ask them for news.
We lit the charred wicks of the lamps
and watched the wind, and listened:
anything could crash and slide away.
Night passed crookedly like nightmare.

Wind blew in my chest.
We'd waited hours for father,
due home on the Beeliner.
Whatever mother feared, I feared.
Maybe the bridge was down.

I thought of the train twisted
off the rails; I couldn't think.
Kerosene glow from the neighbor's window
might have been stars glistening.
They didn't know we were in a frenzy.

I huddled tight in my bones
counting a million by twenties
to bring him home. In my mind,
the train was a Lionel toy,
anyone could smash it.
1000 . . . 1020 . . . 1040 . . .
At midnight the door flew open.
My dazzling father was home, with favors,
red swizzle sticks from the bar car.
I watched him hugging mother,
and heard the wind,
and kept counting.

Dog Days, Sweet Everlasting

Weeks of ninety degree weather—
caniculares dies—
dog days, the Romans said,
certain Sirius the Dog Star
rose with the August sun
and added ferocity to heat.
I bathe every day in the lake
and listen for a rustle, a promise
of rain. A blue sailboat,
becalmed at the island, vibrates
in haze. Black quahog shells
gleam in the wild mint,
dropped there by glutted gulls.

I eat my lunch slowly
under a dark pine,
two tomatoes warm from the sun.

Languid life, writing at night
in damp silence; in the morning,
flopping down like a beached fish
at water's edge, the alewife minnows
and yellow perch swimming discreetly
around me, small bass hovering
darkly nearby in the dock's shade.

I want to live in natural secrecy
a while longer, to be unknown
to myself again, like the catbrier,
savage in its random scratchings—
or like sweet everlasting,
its bristly flower fragrant,
evanescent.

A hummingbird whirs and wavers
in the garden, choosing its honeyed
drink, cosmos or crimson bee
balm. And in an oak tree,
the catbird, clever mimic,
tries several dialects, hoping—
I'm sure it's what he hopes—
to find the song he's given to sing.

Longfellow Park, August

for Lloyd Schwartz

The day is so heavy movement
is nearly impossible; our clothes
stick to our thighs, to the granite
bench—a sweatiness without athletics
or the fever of intimacies.

Across from us, Miles Standish,
Evangeline, and Hiawatha
gaze blankly in *bas relief.*
There are others, too, characters
we're too dazed to name.

The pedestal which held
the bearded poet's bust is empty now,
scarred, a vandalism that's ancient history.
The great yellow mansion
that once stared down to the river
is obscured by maples, and developed lots.
There, his wife met her death by fire.

Those lives were not romances, either.

Afternoons like this leave us limp,
speaking so slowly in the sultriness,
as if the brain kept forgetting its task.
Disappointment emerges like a bruise, slowly,
and the desire to be cared for forever—
character, plot and incident formed
by a proper author.

Friend, we help each other when we can
but today we hide our stickier secrets.
Like *tics douloureux,* our faces ache
from the heat, from bafflement:
we can't revise anyone's life.

Dutch Tulips

The bulbs you smuggled home from Amsterdam
four years ago don't bloom this spring.
Last year, a few brilliant flowers—
perhaps two weeks from start to finish.

You spent your birthday at the Rijksmuseum.
In the damp November cold, I raked leaves
in a fury, digging my bare hands into the icy
piles, the dog shit fossils and dead insects.
I cursed you and our nearest neighbors
calmly bagging the shredded yellow waste.

When you called from Paris, I drove
charges through the transatlantic cable,
one grievance at least for each year
of marriage. Even to myself, I sounded
stupid and selfish. In a post office
phone booth in the *septième arrondissement,*
you were astonished, then hurt and silent.

Each separation then was a divorce,
a permanence I tested, rehearsal of loss
to try my strength. More than anything,
I feared being too domesticated.

I'm no different now.
I still don't forgive the bulbs,
forgive your travelling away.
Or our garden, flaunting
those cheerful inharmonious tulips,
flamboyant stamps on your passport.

Listening to Baseball in the Car

This morning I argued with a friend
about angels. I didn't believe
in his belief in them—I can't
believe they're not a metaphor.
Our argument, affectionate,
lacking in animus, went nowhere.
We promised to talk again soon.
Now, when I'm driving away
from Boston and the Red Sox
are losing, I hear the announcer
say, "No angels in the sky today"—
baseball-ese for *a cloudless afternoon,*
no shadows to help a man
who waits in the outfield
staring into the August sun.
Although I know the announcer's
not a rabbi or sage (no,
he's a sort of sage, disconsolate
philosopher of batting slumps
and injuries), still I scan
the pale blue sky through my
polarized windshield, fervently
hopeful for my fading team
and I feel something a little
foolish, a prayerful throbbing
in my throat and remember

being told years ago that men
are only little lower than
the angels. Floating ahead of me
at the Vermont border, I see
a few wispy horsemane clouds
which I quietly pray will drift
down to Fenway Park where
a demonic opponent has just
slammed another Red Sox pitch,
and the center fielder—call him Jim—
runs back, back, back,
looking heavenward,
and is shielded and doesn't lose
the white ball in the glare.

Two Months in the Country

I

Dawn, and a mourning dove croons
its four notes over and over;
crows caw their harsh pleasures
near the overgrown raspberry beds;
aggressive as Saturday's cartoons,
the loud knock of a woodpecker—

a few identified calls and trills—
what earthly reasons to lie awake
so early in this room over the lake
where mists rise each morning,
and I wait for the day to burn off,

dazzled, as I used to be,
by the blue body, its soft
green shores, and three islands,
three mossy nests waiting
on the cerulean surface—
my lake, opening to me.

. . . But childhood never saw nature
as dazzling, not even the wild
roses, or Lady's Thumbs, not the waxy
Indian Pipes I found yesterday

in the dank woods—like scraps
of paper, or newly dead moths,
but growing, pushing out
through the brown pine needles.

When I was a child, I was told
not to pick or transplant them,
as if there were laws to forbid it.
Colorless as maggots,
they're ugly,
morbid, they felt—prehistoric.

Kingfisher, cormorant, nuthatch —
birds' names come to the tongue,
but my self-consciousness stays.

II

No one's written. The truth
is, I have no address.
Not to say I'm lost, or that
I "lose touch" with reality—

just too indifferent to sink
the heavy post for a mailbox
and learn a new postal etiquette,
the raised red flag . . .

But I have dreams again, thick
black Russian bread, thick white
butter, my grandfather upstairs

again, not dying, lying in a crank
bed, able to love the lake breeze . . .

When you visit, I'm wearing things
differently, raggy shorts, a torn blouse,
my hair wild sticks in the dampness.
I invite you in, but stiffly,

as if I were a hermit
in a tarpaper shed, ragweed
at my door, and enormous purple
thistles, brown spiders
moving on my books.
The sweet smell of honeysuckle,
not success.

Why am I here?
Why stay when loneliness
hollows me in the afternoons,
and at night, gnats, moths,
silent, distant constellations,
and I forget how to work,
except with my hands, in the dirt.

Graves

Mashpee

I.

Mornings, the lake's concealed
by mist. The Canada geese,
who lighted here this season,
are quiet now they've honked
through a wet starless night.

Alone, lazy to a point of stupor,
I think of wrecked vessels
on the Cape beaches, whose "bones,"
as Thoreau wrote, are still
visible jutting from the sand.

Headstones of Praying Indians
lie aslant on my father's land,
mother and son here two centuries.
Once, he took my hand and traced
the willow and urn engraved

on the flaking slabs. I'm losing
him. We both know it, though

we speak the jargon of recovery.
Now, when I gather blueberries
here by the graves, I feel

the old sting of love and heat—
not simple grief—for two
inhabitants of our sometime Eden.
Abandoned souls,
I wanted to protect them,

left berries in a mound
when I was ten, had no prayers
they'd understand, invented
chants and sang to them,
sang to the hallowed ground.

II.

The fog burns off.
The last, breath-holding days of summer,
my "gift for life" is a dim memory,
or a phrase on memory's tongue.
I've been wading through soaked grasses
to a little cemetery three hills,
three scrubby valleys away.
Here, it's always mown,
yet buggy and lonely.
I sit for hours on the damp ground,
hugging myself and deciphering
inscriptions that are eroded, moldy—

Fear, wife of Ellis
1797–18—something
Rest weary one

This must be a kind of perfection,
this proximity to distant deaths.
Before the homely histories,
I don't dwell on the shape
of anyone I love. There's nothing
under these stones, only conventions—
the faintly legible dust
of buried infants, drowned fishermen,
the long stoical lives of widows.
Because I don't want to feel
pity anymore, I study here
where the suffering's remote, antique.

III.

If I could name more constellations
would I be less afraid in the dark,
canoeing on Wakeby Lake? The islands
float like familiar spirits, sweet

and terrifying. *That small wild world . . .*
Ninety feet at its depth, the black
water could quickly take me in
if I'm at all impulsive or clumsy.

I glide uneasily, lit by a gibbous moon,
the day's deep green and dragonfly

blues burnt to charcoal, the white
line of moonlight pulling me through.

Last year, my father fished here.
From shore, I watched the slow drift
of our boat. He'd catch perch or sunnies
and throw them back and go on trolling . . .

I've brought a thermos of coffee
and muffins bleeding with berries
to comfort the chilling night.
Cancer has killed my father's appetite.

What consolation can there be in naming,
or knowing an average star dies quietly?
I've heard of the power of aging stars,
how some go on rampages, radiating

more energy than the sun. Brightest
supernovas, what do they signify?
I look up at the silent inscribed sky—
its dead lights tell a million stories.

Afterward

A week, a month, a year . . .

The rabbi's sister catalogued each stage
of mourning. Half-way through this year,
I still wake sweating to your awful pain.
Or dream you're back with us, weak but intact.

If you were to return, healthy,
a decade younger than your death age—

but those plots make my head reel,
the "ifs" that might have altered history:
"If the plot to murder Hitler had succeeded . . ."

It's only our family history you'd untrack
on its downroad, not the state of nations.

And I'd have spent the last year thinking
of you less—Cordelia, royally accused.

The few illegible notes you left—
a jumbled history—
I still would not have seen.

You never wrote me when I lived away—
that was *my* betrayal. Everyone

else you knew stayed. I fled our Freudian
romance, out until dawn with the jazz musician
you hated, then moved to another state.

More daughter than I'd have chosen,
I feared and miss your loving eye—
my late night guardian, trembling at the door.

To RTSL, 1985

"I'm drained," the last words, I think, you said
to me, four months before your death, the after-reading
crowd at Harvard lingering for a little piece of you.
Is peace to a heroic sufferer possible in the afterlife
promised by yesterday's priest at the latest funeral?
As the congregation rose, responded, and collapsed,
a crazy redhead derelict poked at my neck
with a leathery Book of Common Prayer. I deserved
it, so I didn't turn around to hiss or beg him off—
I didn't love the deceased and shuddered in failed
grief at the homily's stuffy heavenbound platitudes.

In my pew, Jewish mourners snuffled, rebuffed again
at the restricted Gates of Heaven—no everlasting
Paradise for us. Or fear of Hell. You said you wanted
words meat-hooked from the living steer. You'd miss
them in that sermon but sing a fervent Amazing Grace.
Cal, the students come, no less callow or careerist now;
their dented sensibilities might have offended
or amused you no less than Attila's or your son's
babysitter's views. Had you lived beyond that Yellow
Cab ride, you'd be nearly seventy, more frizzled,
your generation's humble chivalrous relentless pride.

Spring Planting

"This is the season
when our friends may and will die daily."
—Robert Lowell, "Soft Wood"

Last year's sunflower stalks blacken
at dusk, their huge exploded suns
droop like the heads of mourners,
frozen in sombre procession.

I carry my seedlings from the car—
snap peas, radishes, an experimental
pole bean . . .
        My little green homunculi,
my hostages to a future season, you've
hardened in April's tonic breeze.

We say you'll bear in so many weeks,
that we'll be here to share the fruit—
it's easy to imagine the future wrong.

The four-year mimosa tree stands pale
and spring-naked, a body's length taller
than last year, and seems to belong.

Years back, at Temple Israel Sunday School
on Saturdays, we donated flattened one-dollar bills
for planting trees in new-born Israel.
Survivors would "make the desert bloom"—
Reform American kids helped prevent erosion.
I imagined dark enormous pines,

my father's sweet name
a plaque on one I'd never find . . .

My friend, your last days among us,
you were such a frail leaf tossing
in pain's hurricane, until morphine
finally took you to sleep with my other
lost ones in a distant forest . . .
                              I place
the flats on the ground by a rusty trowel.
Soon, when the mimosa blossoms again,
its delicate pink blooms will sway
in the Cape's harsh wind, and drop—

oriental creature, its feathery flowers
are evanescent as the colorless smoke
your last cigarette blew across my room.

from **NIGHTFIRE (1978)**

Baseball

The game of baseball is not a metaphor
and I know it's not really life.
The chalky green diamond, the lovely
dusty brown lanes I see from airplanes
multiplying around the cities
are only neat playing fields.
Their structure is not the frame
of history carved out of forest,
that is not what I see on my ascent.

And down in the stadium,
the veteran catcher guiding the young
pitcher through the innings, the line
of concentration between them,
that delicate filament is not
like the way you are helping me,
only it reminds me when I strain
for analogies, the way a rookie strains
for perfection, and the veteran,
in his wisdom, seems to promise it,
it glows from his upheld glove,

and the man in front of me
in the grandstand, drinking banana
daiquiris from a thermos,
continuing through a whole dinner

to the aromatic cigar even as our team
is shut out, nearly hitless, he is
not like the farmer that Auden speaks of
in Breughel's Icarus,
or the four inevitable woman-hating
drunkards, yelling, hugging
each other and moving up and down
continually for more beer

and the young wife trying to understand
what a full count could be
to please her husband happy in
his old dreams, or the little boy
in the Yankees cap already nodding
off to sleep against his father,
program and popcorn memories
sliding into the future,
and the old woman from Lincoln, Maine,
screaming at the Yankee slugger
with wounded knees to break his leg

this is not a microcosm,
not even a slice of life

and the terrible slumps,
when the greatest hitter mysteriously
goes hitless for weeks, or
the pitcher's stuff is all junk
who threw like a magician all last month,
or the days when our guys look
like Sennett cops, slipping, bumping
each other, then suddenly, the play
that wasn't humanly possible, the Kid

we know isn't ready for the big leagues,
leaps into the air to catch a ball
that should have gone downtown
and coming off the field is hugged
and bottom-slapped by the sudden
sorcerers, the winning team

the question of what makes a man
slump when his form, his eye,
his power aren't to blame, this isn't
like the bad luck that hounds us,
and his frustration in the games
not like our deep rage
for disappointing ourselves

the ballpark is an artifact,
manicured, safe, "scene in an Easter egg,"
and the order of the ball game,
the firm structure with the mystery
of accidents always contained,
not the wild field we wander in,
where I'm trying to recite the rules,
to repeat the statistics of the game,
and the wind keeps carrying my words away

—*for John Limon*